Beating the Odds:

A Boyhood Under Nazi-Occupied France

By

George M. Burnell, M.D.

ISBN: 1-4033-5139-2 (e-book)
ISBN: 1-4033-5140-6 (Paperback)
ISBN: 1-4033-5141-4 (Hardcover)

This book is printed on acid free paper.

1stBooks – rev. 08/16/02

To David, Cyndi, Eric, Greg and Robin

To Kevin and those yet unnamed

To Adrienne and Diana

To Dolph and Inge

To Mother

To Don & Fran :
with love, affection
and respect off and
on the t-court
George

La Quinta, October 8, 2002

Table of Contents

Acknowledgments

First and foremost I am especially grateful to Adrienne, my wife, for her constant support, valuable suggestions, helpful critique, and love, without which this book could not have been written.

I am indebted to all those who provided me with interviews and documents and who offered valuable insights while they were still alive: David, Ethel and Betty Distel, Toni and Eddy Wettreich, Opa and Oma Jorysh.

I owe particular thanks to those who filled in the blanks in my memory: Dolph and Inge Wettreich, Fred Sterzer, Irving Malchman, and Lothar Jorysh. Special thanks to Dolph who provided invaluable help with family pictures and with the ones depicting the destruction of Lyon

I owe many thanks for the scores of friends in Santa Clara, Los Gatos, Honolulu, Santa Barbara, and numerous staff members at Kaiser Permanente in Santa Clara and Honolulu who encouraged me to write this book when it was just an idea. Some who merit special mention are Bill and Ardith Huijer, Don and Frances Rockwell, Alex and Colleen Roth.

I am especially indebted to Steve Covington, Public Relations Director at Barnes & Noble in Palm Springs, for his excellent editing, support and wisdom, not to mention his witty comments whenever I reached a low point in the writing.

Finally, I am forever grateful to Mother whose love and support propelled me forward until the day she died.

"The important thing is not to stop questioning."

Albert Einstein

x

Prologue

For the last few years I considered writing a memoir because friends who had heard snippets of my life story urged me to do so. They were fascinated by my tales of survival during Nazi occupied France. "You should write about this. Lots of people would be interested."

I was about to call Cousin Dolph to check out historical details about the family saga during WWII when the phone rang. A warm and pleasant voice was on the other line. It was Cousin Dolph.

"When are you coming to New York?" he asked.

"After Nine Eleven, I'm not sure."

"All is clear now. It's been two months. I must see you," he insisted.

We had not seen each other for over a year. Being the only surviving members of our family, we had become very close and tried to see each other at least once a year.

"I'll get there as soon as I can get a flight," I answered.

I wondered what had triggered the urgency in his voice. I knew that he had not gone to lower Manhattan on that horrible day and thank heaven none of his friends had been caught in that fateful inferno.

A week later he met me at the JFK airport and, as we drove back to the city, he began to relate his problem.

"I've been unable to sleep ever since the attack on the twin towers. Whenever I fall asleep I have these awful dreams about my childhood that keep haunting me and I wake up in a sweat every time. I thought that you, as a psychiatrist, might be able to help me and tell me what's going on."

I know from my training that catastrophic events can trigger dreams and reactivate old life traumas, and that the best way to deal with these phenomena is to talk about these experiences.

"Dolph, we'll have to talk about these dreams and what's behind them," I said.

We arrived at his condo in New Jersey and agreed to go to the Museum of Natural History the next day, our favorite place for a tete a tete.

Dolph was a tall man with grayish hair and a receding hairline. Whenever he spoke he would fix his gaze in my direction as if to make sure that I was giving him my full attention. He had good taste in clothes and took great pride in his appearance. He was a retired businessman who had had a busy and stimulated career in the New York garment industry. He drove us in his Lincoln to the Museum as we had done many times in the past.

We wandered through several exhibits, looking at dinosaurs dating back to 200 million years ago that made us more aware of the passage of time.

We did not engage in small talk. He and I understood how precious time was and we were more interested in bigger issues, such as history, philosophy, art, science, politics and most of all, family stories. Since the death of our parents, we both had a need to "fill in the blanks" of family tales we had never had time to discuss during our working lives.

We settled down at a quiet table in the Museum's restaurant, and I inquired about his disturbing dreams.

"So, tell me about these dreams."

"In one dream, I am in England. I'm thirteen years old. It's cold, dreary, windy, unfriendly and I am shivering. I don't know anyone. Hundreds of children around me are milling around in a makeshift camp. We're all hungry, frightened and huddling in small groups. I'm calling my parents, but no one answers. I'm walking around aimlessly in a maze, unable to find an exit."

Dolph stopped talking when the waiter came and took our orders.

"Now, tell me what was going on in your life when you were a child in the dream?" I asked.

"After Hitler marched into Austria in March 1938, the persecution of Jews became immediate. Life became intolerable. I could no longer go to school without being ridiculed or chased by Hitler youths. Father could no longer work and it was difficult to go shopping. Father was arrested on November 9, which became known as "Crystal Night.""

"What happened then?" I asked.

"That same night the Gestapo stopped my father in the street. They spat on him, called him names and forced him to wash the sidewalk in front of a crowd gathered around to watch him. When he looked up in defiance, they kicked him in the ribs, yelling, "Mach schnell, schweinhund!" (Hurry up, swine)

"My father had been a brave soldier during WWI. He fought the French as a German soldier. He had served his time in the infantry and had been decorated for valor. He was extremely proud of his military record and loved to talk about his war stories."

"Yeah, I remember hearing a few of his stories," I added.

Dolph went on.

"Father was a strong and handsome man who never showed any sign of fear. But in front of these young SS men he couldn't stand up without being kicked down again and again. He was a proud veteran and he refused to ask for mercy and he stared at them as they were hitting him.

"Like thousands of other Jewish men, he was beaten in front of laughing police and indifferent citizens. In dozens of cities in Germany and Austria store windows were shattered and stores were looted in front of local citizens who watched, some in awe, others with approval.

"'Crystal Night', you know, is like Pearl Harbor and Nine Eleven. It's a phrase that is known all over the world. It refers to the glass fragments covering the streets throughout Germany and Austria, glistening like crystals in the light of the street lamps while shop windows were smashed, stores and homes ransacked, and people killed in cold blood.

"You know, George, no Jew could understand what had happened to Germany and Austria where law and order had reigned for generations and where people had felt secure to worship wherever they pleased."

Dolph was talking non-stop. I was enthralled by the story and didn't want to interrupt his train of thought. But Dolph looked at me, concerned that he had talked too much.

"Please go on," I said.

"My mother found out through the Red Cross administration that Father had been sent to Dachau a few days after his arrest. She immediately enrolled as a Red Cross volunteer and was determined to save my father.

"She managed to be assigned to Dachau and once there, she circulated more or less freely within the camp, ministering to various first aid tasks, mostly to the guards and SS men.

"Within a few days, she located my father and saw him in his prisoner's clothes, pitiful, depressed and not the vigorous, proud and happy man she had known all these years. He looked dazed, had a vacant stare and walked aimlessly around his barrack.

"As Mother approached him, he didn't recognize her in her Red Cross uniform. She whispered in his ear, 'It's me. Toni. Listen and listen good. You must hang on, Eddy. I'll get you out of here. Don't answer. Just nod.' He looked up, nodded and shuffled away like an old man.

"Mother had connections with a group of Chinese individuals who knew how to manufacture false papers including visas, passports, exit documents, birth certificates and anything that one could afford to buy. She obtained exit papers with Father's name and valid visas which she gave to the camp officials through channels. My mother, like your mother, was very resourceful, you know."

"Yes, I know," I said.

"Ten months later, as she had promised, Father was released and rejoined Mother in Vienna. With their papers in hand they immediately left Austria and reached England in August 1939, one month before the declaration of war.

I was fascinated by the story. I urged him to go on.

"After my father reached England, there was a wave of propaganda that had been instigated by German sources. The rumor was that many Jews coming to England had been trained as spies for the Fifth column, a German spy ring which had infiltrated foreign countries. Special makeshift tribunals were established to handle this particular problem. Jewish refugees were classified as possible *enemy aliens* or *friendly aliens*. Ironically, Father was classified as enemy alien, a spy suspect, and was held prisoner in the Isles of Man Camp and housed with German pilots who had been shot down over England.

"I have no idea why Mother was classified as *friendly alien* and was allowed to reside in the community at large. Without wasting any time, she managed to obtain an affidavit for the United States after befriending an American doctor who had been on a personal mission to save European Jews.

"One day a guard in the camp where Father was staying told him to get ready to go to the ship that was leaving for the United States the following day.

"On the same day, Mother received the message that she was to report for embarkation on the S.S. Warwick Castle headed to the U.S. She didn't know of Father's or my whereabouts.

"She went to the dock where the boat was anchored. Father saw her walking up the plank. When she stepped on board, Father and Mother fell into each other's arms and wept tears of joy. The first thing she asked was, "Where is Dolphy?"

Father said that he heard that there was a contingent of children from the KinderTransport aboard, and perhaps I would be among them. My parents walked by hundreds of children, asking, "Have you seen a boy named Dolphy? A big, strong boy?" Finally, Mother spotted me first in a group of quiet children standing on a lower deck and ran towards me, shouting, "Dolphy. 'Dolphy. My God. I'm so happy I found you. Look over here. Your father is here too."

Dolph was almost out of breath as he related this episode, but he went on.

"We all embraced and hugged for several minutes until an official tapped us on the shoulder and said, 'It's time to go to your cabin and process your papers. You'll meet again later.'

"Father's incarceration had been the basis for my being considered immediately eligible for evacuation to England. I was thirteen years old then. The project was called the *KinderTransport*. Frankly, I don't remember anything about the crossing to England."

"You're doing well. Please go on," I said.

"I arrived in London in December 1938 and was taken to a camp for Jewish children. The officials asked if I wanted to stay with an *adoptive family* but I refused. So they sent me to the Linksfield Camp for *enemy aliens*."

"Wouldn't it have been better to go with a family?" I asked.

"In my heart I felt that I would see Mother and Papa again. I didn't want any other mama or papa."

"And then what happened?"

Dolph's face was tense and he leaned over as if he didn't want anyone else to hear what he had to say. He sighed and his face relaxed. It was as if a huge weight had been lifted off his shoulders.

He sat back and his head and shoulders lifted gently from the slumped posture.

"Believe me, George. I haven't told this story to anyone before. It's as if a tight knot has been loosened inside my chest."

I smiled, put my hand on his shoulder and said, "I'm so glad you did, Dolph."

In the days that followed, he reported that the nightmares had vanished and that he was again sleeping peacefully.

*   *   *

Dolph had told me as much as he knew about the KinderTransport. But being curious about the history of that project, I wanted to know more and did some research of my own.

In 1938, Britain had announced that it was willing to extend a temporary haven to Jewish children living under Nazi oppression.

Thought to be a rumor at first, the rumor had become a reality.

Why had England made such an offer? A number of circumstances had come into play. First, there was Kristallnacht (Crystal Night, November 9, 1938) which had shaken the indifference of governments. People began to clamor, "If the adults cannot be saved, at least save the children."

Second, The public outcry to help those children encouraged the British government and the House of Commons to permit Jewish children to seek refuge in Great Britain.

Two conditions had to be met:

1/ The children had to be under eighteen years of age and 2/ They had to be certified to be healthy. The British envisioned that the stay of these children would be temporary and that a guarantee of fifty pounds per child for possible re-migration was required. Many organizations went into action, pledged the money, found guarantors and battled bureaucratic obstacles. They also collected goods for the children and found places where they could stay.

That was only half of the solution. One had to deal with the German emigration officials, who had to grant permission for the children's departure. The official-in-charge was in Vienna and his name was Adolf Eichmann, not an easy man to deal with.

One of the originators of the Refugee Children's Movement, Norman Bentwich, knew the right person for the task: Gertrude Wijsmuller, a Dutch woman who had been active in refugee affairs.

As soon as she was appointed to carry out this mission, she left for Vienna, demanded an interview with Eichmann and explained to him that the British Government was willing to accept 10,000 Jewish children. Eichmann's reaction was scornful. Why was she, an Aryan, bothering about Jewish children? Undaunted, she persisted. Finally Eichmann agreed to let 600 children go.

A train was made available and the rescue project became known as the KinderTransport. Fifty years later those children who were rescued still refer to themselves as Kinder. In his zeal to obstruct further, Eichmann made an additional condition: all the 600 children had to be out of the country within five days!

*   *   *

Dolph was most grateful to have regained peace of mind and the pleasure of restful sleep. A week later, he drove me to the airport and, before we said our goodbyes, he said, "What about that memoir you've been talking about? It's about time for people to hear the story of how you survived in Nazi-occupied France."

1- Strasbourg

In 1939 Strasbourg was a beautiful, peaceful and happy city. For two thousand years it sat quietly by the Rhine, embraced by the two arms of the Ill river at the crossroads of Europe, where hundreds of armies had marched back and forth after defeat or victory.

Nowadays tourists crowd the city to see the beautiful Cathedral of Notre Dame which has been standing since the 14th century, displaying her red stone facade of Gothic lace work and elaborate stainglass windows and sculptures.

When one walks through the streets of Strasbourg, it's as if one is treated to a smorgasbord of the senses. The Hofbrau signs are everywhere. In the air one can smell the aroma of the sauerkraut and pork chops cooking in all the kitchens. In the cobbled stone streets, it's irresistible to stop by the pastry shops and see in the windows colorful little fruit tarts and beautiful Gugelhupfts (a light pound cake) sprinkled with snowy sugar powder and red, white and brown gingerbread Santa Clauses in small and big sizes. High up the church bells are tolling as beautiful maidens dressed in their Alsatian costumes smile as they pass by.

At the end of the day, workers sing their favored tunes in beer halls and after dinner they dance in the bistros where accordions, violins and pianos fill the air with old Alsatian tunes.

In 1939 it was no different than it had been in years past except that while all these joyful, peaceful and happy celebrations were going on, no one suspected that across the Kehl bridge on the Rhine, Germany, like a sleeping leopard, was waiting to pounce and kill again.

*   *   *

Tucked away behind the Strasbourg Cathedral, in a very narrow street, was the building where Papa, Mother and I lived. The street was named "rue du ciel", which means street of heaven. My guess was that some of the local folks believed that the path to heaven was behind the cathedral and those who lived there probably were "insiders" with the holy spirits.

I tried to play on "Heaven's street" but the kids of the neighborhood would gang up against me. They called me "Frenchie", which I imagined was their way of telling me that I was different from them. They spoke Alsatian, a Germanic dialect, and they were of Germanic descent and culture. Their sympathies lay with the German people across the bridge.

Hans was my only friend. His family was Alsatian but he didn't know how his family felt about our friendship. He explained to me that although his grandfather was born French, he became German when in 1871 Alsace was taken over by Germany after the Franco-Prussian War. His grandfather again changed nationality in 1918 at the end of World War I and became French again. Now, his father who was French was saying that when Germany wins this next war, the family will become German again. This all sounded confusing to Hans and he didn't know what to do about our friendship. I remember Hans saying to me, 'Even my friends don't want me to talk to the 'Frenchie'.

At home life was beautiful. We had a chauffeur who doubled up as a gardener, handyman and jack-of-all-trades, a big house with most of the conveniences of the time, including a radio, a phonograph, bicycles, and attractive modern mahogany furniture.

My parents owned a hotel and restaurant which catered mostly to tourists who came from all over Europe. Mother ran the restaurant, supervised the kitchen, directed the waitresses and welcomed the customers. Father supervised the hotel staff and took care of supplies, repairs, deliveries and city permits.

It was all well-orchestrated and organized and life was orderly, pleasant and peaceful.

Father, and Mother were busy in their own world, and like most of the folks then, they talked about the weather, politics, the neighbors, the business world and whatever grown folks talk about.

People also talked about a new German dictator, Adolph Hitler, who had annexed the Rhineland, marched into Austria, invaded Czechoslovakia and later Poland. Most people said he was just an annoyance and a nuisance, a temperamental fool, who eventually would soon disappear and fizzle out.

I lived in my own little world. I kept to myself and had plenty of games for amusement. Although I was an only child, the ghost of my dead twin brother still remained in my mind, and I felt a mysterious presence even when I was playing alone.

I did not speak the Alsatian dialect nor did I wish to learn it.

My mother seemed fluent in Alsatian and could switch back and forth between Alsatian and French almost within the same sentence. She was also fluent in "hoch Deutch", the pure German of Northern Germany, which was to come handy later on.

I discovered that I wasn't welcome in the Alsatian community. I never admitted it until I faced the truth.

One day, while riding my bike in the neighborhood, a car raced by and hit me broadside. I fell off the bike. Everything became a blur after I landed in a tangle of chains, wheels and steel frame.

I remember lying helpless in a pool of blood, all sprawled out in the middle of the street. Despite the pain, I had desperately tried to hold back my tears. Then I had heard some people say, 'It's the Frenchie. Don't bother. Someone will come for him.'

After a half hour during which I could have bled to death, my father finally arrived and took me to the local emergency room for stitching of my ear, which was barely hanging on the side of my head. I learned that an anonymous caller had reached my father, who was furious. "How could they do this, leaving you like this in the middle of the street? These people are barbaric!"

He was always quick to turn any adverse event into a lecture. "Let that be a lesson to you. You can't trust them. You've got to be more careful and not expect any help from anyone out there. They are all the same. They hate the French, so don't forget it."

I learned to handle situations on my own. I didn't want any more lectures or reprimands. I would face my enemies as a lone warrior.

One day, after the beginning the school term, I was ambushed by a gang of boys who yelled "Come over here Frenchie. We'll show you who is king here!"

As they encircled me, a tall fat boy, posing as their leader, gave the order to throw stones in my direction, while two older boys approached with their fists ready to strike.

I saw a slight opening in the group and made a dash toward my house. I ran along side streets and along the buildings like a thief being chased until I reached my house. It was then that I realized that I was bleeding from my forehead. I swore that some day I would become a martial arts expert and hold my own with those thugs.

"What happened to you?" Mother said, as she saw me coming through the front door.

"Oh, it's nothing. I just fell down in the school yard. I'll go wash myself."

Even with Mother, I had learned not to complain because she would get hysterical and eventually upset my father.

In the classroom, I learned to survive from the abuse of teachers, especially those who had a built-in hatred of the French. One teacher, Mr. Himmler, loved to call on me when no one knew the answer to his questions. On one such day, he called on me. "Well, let's see how smart is that French boy" he bellowed in his strong Alsatian accent, showing his crooked teeth behind a sardonic grin, "George, do you know who invaded France before Charlemagne?"

At first, I froze. I was at a loss for an answer. He added, "Come here, George, and show the class your lovely hands. Now, squeeze your finger tips together so I can warm them up with this fine ruler and help refresh your memory."

Dumbfounded and silent, I stood still in front of the class. After a few seconds, he raised the ruler high up in the air and, with amazing accuracy, landed ten strong hits on the fingers of my right hand and then repeated the cruel punishment on the fingers of my left hand. The skin turned red and blood oozed between my fingers.

"Go back to your seat. And do better next time you're called on," said Himmler, while nodding to the class.

I dreaded going back to his classes, but didn't want to make trouble.

I learned to show my bravery by holding back my tears and remaining silent. I fantasized plunging a dagger into his chest.

It was then that I concluded that it wasn't such a good idea to be French. The alternative of being German seemed totally abhorrent to me.

I kept thinking that some day we would leave the country and not be French anymore.

"Do we have to be French?" I asked Mother.

Sensing my unease and tension, she would look at me with her big brown smiling eyes and take me in her arms.

"Don't worry, George. Some day, we'll move and everything will be all right."

Mother always seemed to look out for me. I knew that I was the most important person in her life, and she often told me that I was. She seemed so concerned about my welfare that I made sure not to upset her with my complaints, aches or pains.

Her greatest hope was that I get a proper education. She insisted that I go to school every day, not aware, since I never told her, that school was a war zone for me. I never shared with her the problems I had had with Mr. Himmler for fear that she wouldn't have understood or believed me.

Child abuse, in those days, was not a well-understood concept, and teachers were kings and queens in their classrooms. There was no court of appeals for pupils or students who were mistreated by teachers.

As soon as I'd get home, Mother would ask the same question she had asked the day before "George, did you learn anything today?"

"Yes, Mother. French history has many twists and turns and it does *strike* me as funny sometimes."

She seemed satisfied with my schoolwork, although I wondered whether she suspected that school was not always a pleasant experience for me. But if she did, she chose not to interfere or pry into my scholastic world. Whenever she sensed my discouragement at the end of the day, she'd come through with soothing words of support and love, and a final message, "George, whatever you do, whatever you think, whatever you fear, you must stay in school."

* * *

Across the Rhine was a vast region of West Germany called the Rhineland, where the powerful industrial cities of Cologne,

Dusseldorf, Essen and Saarbrucken provided the steam, coal, oil and steel that was needed by Germany.

Following World War I, the region had been occupied from 1918 to 1930 by Allied troops. The Rhineland had been designated a demilitarized "buffer zone" between Germany and France by the Treaty of Versailles. In total defiance, Hitler had started to build up the army presence in that area.

He reminded the German people that France, on November 11, 1919, the date of the signing of the Treaty of Versailles, had stolen Alsace Lorraine from the German people. "It was time to get it back, to get revenge and to redress from a terrible injustice to the Reich, which is the land of the superior race," he would bellow in his speeches.

The French, who had watched this military build-up for several years, had chosen to ignore it. Knowing this, Hitler had forged ahead with his plans to continue the arms race to equip his army, air force and navy. He said that he would be ready to tackle and overcome any country in Europe.

On the morning of March 7, 1936, Hitler, without warning, sent his soldiers with drums and flags flying into the region, seven days after the President of the United States, Franklin D. Roosevelt, had signed the second Neutrality Act!

Although reoccupation of the Rhineland was a violation, not only of the Versailles treaty, but also of America's separate peace treaty with Germany of 1921 and the Locarno Pact of 1925. Secretary of State Cordell Hull didn't raise a note of protest, and FDR went fishing that day.

The French and British had protested, but hadn't even moved a single soldier. It was a fateful moment. The French army, then more powerful than the German, could easily have ejected the three battalions carrying out the ceremonial reoccupation of the Rhineland.

Hitler's invasion reinforced the idea that Western democracies were populated by an inferior race, genetically damaged, contaminated by Jews and Blacks. As he said over and over, these inferior people were lazy, preoccupied with getting rich, making Hollywood movies, producing stupid phonograph records, and promoting beauty queens.

Hitler got the signal from these democracies that now was the time to proceed with his plans to dominate the rest of Europe and perhaps the world.

2- Mother and Father

Mother never took any vacations and couldn't understand why some people did. Perhaps she and Father couldn't afford it although I believe that taking time for relaxation was not part of their lifestyle.

I suppose her way of looking at leisure time put an imprint on my psyche because when I'm on vacation I have to make a conscious effort to relax or allow myself to pass the time without a defined purpose or goal. I had to convince Mother and myself that going on vacation was not only useful, but had to be educational, enriching and worthwhile.

Although Mother never was tidy, she always found the things she was looking for. She never dressed elegantly but she was always presentable in public. She was proud of her efficiency and especially of her good credit and, because she never owed anyone any money, she was a dream customer at all the banks in the city.

When she reached 40, she developed a medical problem that would change the rest of her life. It was a condition diagnosed as "plantar warts" which essentially were warts that grew inwardly inside the sole of the feet. These warts, caused by a "virus" (although it was not known at the time) grow "tentacles" deep inside the flesh under the feet.

No one knows why anyone gets this condition which affects only certain susceptible individuals.

With today's medical knowledge this problem is relatively easy to treat by injecting a substance which infiltrates the warts and burns them chemically.

But in the 1940s, because this condition was not well-understood, doctors advised surgical removal of these growths which were spreading throughout the sole of her feet like cancerous tumors. She consulted the best surgeon in town, who eventually removed them.

The surgery left thick and ugly scars on the ball of her feet, which were even more painful than the original lesions.

The next medical consultant suggested that burning the scars with radiation would eliminate the problem. But after the scars were burned with high doses of radiation, the burned flesh became even more painful than the surgical scars had been.

Mother consulted dermatologists, who recommended a variety of salves; orthopedists, who recommended special shoes with holes dug out where the burns existed; and internists, who suggested narcotics. When she became depressed, her doctors prescribed anti-depressants and when she became anxious, restless, and unable to sleep, they prescribed sedatives and tranquilizers. She lived with a complete pharmacy at her bedside. Some medications would pep her up, others would bring her down, while others would numb her feet or her mind.

She never wore the elegant and fashionable shoes that most women adore to wear. Her shoes were open-toed and seemed to fit her awkwardly. She stopped taking long walks and always calculated distances before shopping, traveling or keeping business or medical appointments.

Consultants began to think that her pain was "all in her mind." For years, I suspected that doctors' treatment failures are often attributed to patient's "weak minds" and diagnosed as "psychosomatic problems."

Mother gradually became burdened with recurring depressive moods that would sap her energy and optimism for months at a time.

Doctors would prescribe Dexamyl, a combination of dexedrine and phenobarbital, which she took for years and to which she eventually became addicted.

*   *   *

My father was a tall, handsome and athletic-looking man, who never played any team sports or games. Yet, he was broad-shouldered, had strong Samson-like legs, and a chest that could have been the envy of the best body builders.

He sported an Errol Flynn mustache and had a full head of dark black hair, smiling brown eyes, and could have made a living as a male model for fitness or men's fashion magazines.

He loved to sing arias from the most well-known operas like Carmen, Aida, and Tosca. Mother used to say, "I loved that man's voice. That's how I fell in love with him."

She also admired his amazing knowledge and skill for repairing anything that fell apart in the house. He was a master electrician, painter, plumber, carpenter, mason, mechanic: a true jack-of-all-trades.

How could she have resisted such an array of talents? And I wondered how anyone could know so much? He had been trained as a master machinist and enjoyed the challenge of repairing anything that failed to function.

I was in awe of him most of the time. I remember him in his long beige overalls, whistling or singing operas while tinkering, sawing, hammering, screwing, painting, or simply putting away his tools. He had a tool shop and a workbench that would have been the pride of any professional craftsman.

He often let me watch while he repaired toilets, painted the house or installed new wiring in the walls and ceilings. I felt like a little dog, sitting next to his master, expected to show respect and awe at this display of blue collar talent. Yet, he never offered to teach me any of the skills. I wondered if he thought I was too dumb or too clumsy.

I believe that my aversion for fixing anything around the house later in life was a reaction to this negatively charged experience. Now,

I don't even like to watch a plumber or an electrician repair things when they come to the house.

I felt that Father and Mother were a good team, he with his manual skills and she with her business sense. It was a perfect match and a good recipe for success in their new venture of running a hotel and restaurant in Strasbourg.

Mother was the dominant business brain in that partnership. They argued constantly over how much money should be spent on various business items, but in the end they seemed to work it out. They wanted to please the guests in the hotel and strive for excellence.

*   *   *

The hotel also attracted non-human guests who gathered in the corridors, the roof and the courtyard. These were all the cats of the neighborhood who enjoyed roaming through the "Eureka Hotel."

Like many of our guests, they were taking advantage of the luxurious surroundings for making love in the middle of the night. In the act of mating, being louder that human guests, they would make deafening wailing sounds that would echo throughout the entire hotel.

Exasperated, my father, would crawl out of bed, take his gun, and go on the prowl, ready to shoot the first cat he could sight. I would jump out of bed, out of a sound sleep, while gunshots were exploding up and down the staircase and throughout the hotel.

Was he trying to teach them a lesson too, so they shouldn't be as careless and trusting as I was?

The next day, I would rejoice when I learned that not a single cat had been hit, but found that bullet holes on the walls would need to be filled and plastered, a task that would keep Father occupied for days. Mother would yell at him, "What will our customers think when they see all these bullet holes in the walls?"

My father was in love with France and undoubtedly would have given his life for his country. How was he to know that before long he would be called upon to fight to prove his true loyalty and to live up to his ideal.

He loved to give lectures which he called his "lessons in living." I think he loved me in his own way, but I felt that his love was conditional on my staying out of trouble and on my good performing in school…no small task, given the political climate of the school environment.

Like many fathers of his generation, he believed that if I couldn't understand his sermons, the best way was to pound them into me.

He had the knack of landing his open hand on my face with the precision of a professional boxer. I learned reflex ducking. It never did any good, but it left me with good reflexes that helped me in future fights.

I wondered why my face was always in the trajectory of his open hand. I figured out that there were several steps in the learning process. The first was to listen carefully to loud instructions. If the instructions didn't provide the desired results, the second step was the open hand across my face. If that failed, the third and final step was to send me down into the cellar for an hour or two.

There, I learned to introspect at an early age and to cope with the cold, damp and dark environment of the basement. I learned that mice were friends of mankind and never would harm a helpless child. But I also wondered what kind of father would treat his son this way? Was it really fatherly love? Did other fathers punish their sons in this way? I swore to myself that if I ever had a son, I would never subject him to such barbaric abuse.

I also wondered what Mother was thinking about each time he sent me down to the cellar. Was she on my side or on his side? Was she afraid to stand up to him? She never expressed an opinion on the matter but for years I wondered how she really felt about it. Regardless, I never doubted her love for me.

3- War

Hitler marched into Austria in March, 1938. He had agitated for the Anschluss, the union of the two countries, Germany and Austria, during the 1920s and early 30s, ignoring the WWI Treaty of Versailles, which he had violated. The Nazi parties had become well-entrenched in both countries and in 1934, Austrian Nazis murdered Chancellor Dollfuss in an attempted coup to overthrow the government. The coup failed. In February, 1938, Hitler summoned the new Austrian Chancellor Shuschnigg to Berchtesgaden.

During the meeting, Hitler intimidated the Chancellor and demanded the reinstatement of the Austrian Nazi party, which had been banned in Vienna.

Schuschnigg felt helpless and frightened, but tried one more attempt at resistance by calling a referendum on the issue of uniting the two countries. Hitler continued to pressure for the unification of the two countries and by March 11, the referendum was cancelled.

The next day, German troops marched into Austria, and Gestapo and SS troops began their brutal suppression by arresting, kidnapping or murdering dignitaries and ordinary people. Shuschnigg was one of the first of 76,000 Austrians sent to Dachau in the early weeks of the Anschluss.

As the terror continued, an Austrian concentration camp was established at Mathausen where another 35,000 people were executed.

Following this wave of brutality, Hitler called for another vote on April 10th. Austrians went to the polls and 99 per cent voted in favor of the annexation.

In September, 1938, British Prime Minister Neville Chamberlain was invited to have tea with Adolf Hitler at his Berchtesgaden hideaway.

The two men shook hands and signed a paper which allowed Germany to absorb the Sudetenland part of Czechoslovakia. This agreement, incidentally, also met with FDR's approval as well as that of his ambassador in London, Joseph Kennedy. They felt that Hitler had a good argument because he said that he was redressing the grievances of the 3.5 million Germans in the Sudetenland.

In October, Chamberlain made two more trips to Germany and agreed to the so-called Munich agreement, which gave the green light to Hitler to send his troops into the entire region bordering Czechoslovakia. On March 15, 1939, Hitler took over the whole of Czechoslovakia, breaking his promise to respect the independence of the non-German regions, ignoring his excuse that he had acted solely on behalf of his German minority. Europe was still in a total state of denial. Hitler was measuring his steps one at a time while at the same time appeasing the rest of the world around him.

Only one man seemed to have awakened to the distant sounds of the marching divisions and roaring tanks: Winston Churchill. Uneasy and restless, he had sounded the alarm when he said, "Do not suppose this is the end; this is only the beginning of the reckoning."

* * *

Older generations remember the bloody ravages the German ogre had caused when it had crossed the Khel bridge over the Rhine river during the Great War, 'WWI'. Now, in the Fall of 1939, there was an uneasy feeling in the air that the ogre might be ready to attack again, but the French Government chose to ignore the signals, thinking that the climate of uncertainty resulted from German propaganda spreading fear and panic.

The government wanted to present a face of confidence. But confidence was a thin veneer and behind the scenes there were deep misgivings. Many people felt that their leaders were more interested in playing politics than preparing for war. In the face of the Germany's nonaggression pact with the Soviet Union, some people felt that France had targeted the wrong enemy. "Hitler is bad, but Stalin is worse," they said. French foreign policy was highly suspect, and as one historian put it, it was torn "constantly between defeatist panic and aggressive overconfidence."

Prime Minister Daladier believed that a defensive strategy based on the Maginot Line was the best way to protect France and prevent a war. He rejected the views of a tank commander named Charles de Gaulle who argued that France's hopes depended on the creation of a career army based on powerful and mobile armored forces. Even after Daladier was replaced by the more aggressive Paul Reynaud, de Gaulle's strategy was still ignored.

It is ironic that young German commanders had read all the books de Gaulle had written on motorized mobile units and had incorporated his ideas on offensive-oriented strategy into their own army.

Another explanation for the government's reluctance and apathy could be understood if one remembered the terrible wastage of young men in 1914-18, which had made France a nation of mutilated veterans, old people and cripples. By the middle 1930s young men eligilible for the draft dropped in half because so few boys had been born in 1915-19.

To make matters worse there was a continuing power struggle between Prime Minister Reynaud and Edouard Daladier, the man he had replaced and was now Foreign Minister. Daladier insisted on a defensive approach while Reynaud favored a more aggressive one.

On September 3, 1939, Germany declared war. France was shaken out of its torpor initially, but then went back to bed for more snoozing, thinking that its restless neighbor would eventually come to its senses and renege on its threats.

After war was declared, nothing happened. There were no battles, no threats from Berlin, no talk of counterattack. Just a few planes flying leisurely over Paris. French forces made a halfhearted attempt to penetrate the German front but quickly fell back to more secure positions behind the Maginot Line, confident that the fortifications which ran from Switzerland to the Luxembourg and Belgian borders would provide sufficient protection. These fortifications which had been built between the two wars were thought to be a deterrence against any German attack into France. The Maginot Line was a symbol of France's policy of defensive thinking.

Most people felt if Germany did attack, France was fully prepared. "Confidence is a duty!" newspapers reported. Even the advertising department of a major store in the fall of 1939 proclaimed: "Madame, it is your duty to be elegant!" In Paris restaurants were crowded and there were long lines in front of movie houses. "Paris must remain Paris," clamored Maurice Chevalier, "so that soldiers on leave can find a bit of Parisian charm despite all."

At the Maginot Line soldiers were bored from inactivity. Even four months after the war had been declared, nothing had happened. To kill time, some soldiers took up gardening and planted rosebushes along the Maginot Line. Others took their binoculars to peer across the border, placing bets while watching Germans play soccer.

In April 1940, seven months since the war had been declared, sidewalk cafes in Paris were full. It was as if prosperity, gaiety and hospitality were back as usual in the spring. People were waiting and wondering what Germany might do and behaving as if it were business as usual. This period of inaction was called *la drole de guerre* or Phony War.

No one suspected that it would soon end except in Alsace-Lorraine where people were fatalistic, remembering the repeated invasions of the past. Between 1870 and 1940, these provinces had changed hands twice, passing from France to Germany (1879), and from Germany back to France (1918). Each time Alsatians had to change their nationality which meant that people were part French part German, but most of all Alsatian.

With the declaration of war, the French government feared an attack from the German army and ordered the city of Strasbourg, located just across the Rhine River from Germany, be evacuated. A few weeks later when nothing had happened, most of the 200,000 residents had returned, thinking that it had been a false alarm.

Many people believed that with the signing of the Munich agreement everything would be all right. A few of our friends, however, thought otherwise. They did not trust Hitler when he signed a friendship and nonaggression pact with the Soviet Union in August 1939. They had a sense of foreboding as threatening as an oncoming storm, and felt that Germany could only be stopped if the United States joined the war. But all hopes vanished when, in October, President Roosevelt affirmed that he would abide by the Neutrality Act.

Over the following months a feeling of gloom pervaded the whole region. Many thought it would be their last Christmas as French citizens and elderly men did not want to die as Germans. Young men too young to be drafted into the French army dreaded being called into the German army.

* * *

Little did the French people know that the pending world war was going to be the greatest single tragedy mankind had ever known. All because the French, like the British and the Americans, believed in a policy of "containment". The British leadership of the day thought appeasement would buy peace.

On May 9 Hitler said to his staff, "Gentlemen, you are about to witness the most famous victory in history."

The following day, German forces, using some of the very tactics advocated by Charles de Gaulle, breached the Meuse and made their way through the heavily wooded Ardennes, bypassing the Maginot Line.

The French army was overwhelmed. Though it had more tanks, they were spread out and ineffective. Yet, as one soldier said, "We can beat the Boches and have it over by autumn."

Little did he know that it would be over much sooner.

* * *

Could a world war have been prevented? Yes!! When Hitler devoured Czechoslovakia, the combination of France, Britain and the United States, with or without the Soviet Union, could easily have imposed peace or defeated him in a short war.

This is why, I think, that the responsibility for the great tragedy that followed must be shared by all of these countries.

It was not just the politics of isolationism in America that was responsible for the inertia, but also the fact that the Western countries were not interested in getting help from the United States.

* * *

Meanwhile, in other parts of Europe, there was a rapid development of events. Mussolini's troops had invaded Albania. Stalin had invaded Finland without declaration of war. Hitler had invaded Poland and had captured 900,000 Polish soldiers, sending half of them to concentration camps. He also had rounded up 3.2 million Jews into ghettos, and had sent 550,000 of them in the first convoy to various concentration camps. In the first month after the invasion German forces claimed more than 10,000 lives, including 3,000 Polish Jews, some of whom were forced into synagogues and burned alive.

That was the prelude to more cataclysmic happenings to come.

*   *   *

When war broke out, I remember my mother saying, "France and England declared war on Germany! They want to stop Germans from coming here and taking all our things."

My father, like a true French patriot, had said "Ces sales Boches, ils ont du culot!"("these dirty krauts, they have some nerve!") It was all right for the Germans to take Austria, Czechoslovakia and Poland, but not France. That was inconceivable and nervy!

Father had gone on and on, muttering, "Ca ne va pas durer; ces salots, ils vont regretter toute cette histoire!' (They won't last long, those bastards; they'll be sorry about the whole thing.)

Everyone in France had the same feeling and attitude. People would say, "These krauts won't last. We'll kick them back so fast they won't know what hit them. They'll never get through the Maginot Line!"

As a child, I had played with toy lead soldiers, making out various war scenarios. I'd pretend that I was a general, ordering one division to the right, one division to the left and a token force to face the enemy in front to feign a full fledged attack.

As I read accounts of the WWII battles fought in Europe, I learned that generals in the field played the same games, although this time with live soldiers.

So, I wouldn't have to play with pretend armies, tanks and soldiers' anymore, I'd see real tanks, real cannons, and real fighter planes!

"Are we going to leave the country?" I asked Mother, thinking that my political troubles with the neighborhood kids and schoolteachers might be over. She didn't answer, but I understood years later that it was not as stupid a question as it might have seemed. The idea of leaving the country then was totally foreign and unacceptable to my parents.

Nevertheless, I heard them debate a number of questions. Should we leave Strasbourg? Was it going to be dangerous to stay? Could anyone rely on the popular opinion that the threats of danger were exaggerated? After all, there was the Maginot Line, an indestructible and impenetrable wall which had been built after the bitter defeat of WWI. No army would ever have the capability of piercing through this wall. So, why leave?

4- Opa and Oma

The day after Hitler took possession of Austria, he closed all the borders and issued the order to forbid Jews to leave the country.

Grandfather Opa and Grandmother Oma, who were living in Vienna, had just missed their last chance to leave. Father, Mother and I shuddered at the thought that they were caught in this web of terror.

I had such fond memories of Opa and Oma, having spent two years of my early childhood at their home in Vienna. I still remember their mannerisms, their gaze, their winning smiles, their gentle touch, and most of all their hugs and kisses.

Oma was a petite woman with dark silky hair, beautiful white skin, a thin body, and a gentle Mona Lisa smile. Her voice was muffled and slurred, because of partial deafness believed to be the result of a fall in infancy. She had simple tastes, wore no makeup, never spent money on herself, was kind, affectionate, and totally dedicated to doing housework and cooking.

She loved to cook "latkes" (pancakes made with potatoes, onions, eggs, and matzo meal cooked with oil, usually eaten with apple sauce) and bake "strudel" because she knew how much I liked them.

I remember watching her in the kitchen while the sweet aroma of sizzling latkes in the hot skillet was making my mouth water. She looked happy and was smiling as she was shaping the potato mixture in her hands before throwing it into the boiling oil.

She also made "gefilte fish" (small fish balls eaten with horse radish'chrain, which is judged in its relative strength in bringing tears to the eyes) and blintzes (the Jewish answer to crepe suzette). Opa used to say that Oma cooked with love in her heart and goodness in her soul. This was true.

Opa was a tall, slender, robust, handsome man with a twinkle in his eyes, thinning white hair and a receding hairline. Even though he didn't practice any sport, he was extremely muscular and stood erect, holding his head high like a military officer.

He loved bagels and when I asked "Why the hole?" he would say, "Philosophers believe the hole is the essence and the dough is only there for emphasis!"

He did have a nasty habit. He seemed to delight in launching the loudest, the most strident, the most grating farts Man is capable of producing as if these were weapons in his arsenal.

I figured out the secret way he manufactured his farts. He would cook "cholent", a Jewish version of refried Mexican beans except that its gas-producing power is far greater than the Mexican version.

Cholent is a combination of beans, barley, potatoes and bones or meat, which will form a large bolus in the pit of the stomach. If you cook cholentburgers for your guests, you are guaranteed never to see them again!

Father, Mother and I wondered what they could do to escape. We were soon to find out.

They arrived at the border, taking their chances that something miraculous would happen in their favor. They spoke German to an official of the border patrol, explaining that they had an urgent call to attend sick relatives in France. The official listened, asked them to wait in an isolation room. He came back half an hour later, explaining that the crossing would be possible, but that they would have to pay a substantial fee and that they would agree never to come back. They agreed to these conditions and handed over a significant amount of cash. The officer waved them on without even requesting to see their identity papers, visa or passport. There are times in life when one has to take the risk with the hope of beating the odds. And so they crossed into France.

Opa and Oma traveled from Austria to Switzerland, then over to Alsace, finally reaching us in Strasbourg. Because German was spoken in all these places, they were able to negotiate effectively.

They told us how frightened and humiliated they had felt, but despite their distress, they managed not to panic, determined to rejoin their children on the other side of the border.

Their arrival in Strasbourg was an emotional event. We all embraced, saying, "Thank God. Thank God, you are here, safe and sound."

Mother said with tears in her eyes, "And that's all that counts."

Opa and Oma didn't speak French, but spoke to me in their Austrian dialect. They looked so happy to be reunited with Mother and with me, having been apart for more than four years.

*   *   *

As my father prepared to leave for the front, Opa became the new male figure to look up to. He was about six feet tall and stood erect like a soldier. He had fought in the infantry on the German side in WWI, had a twinkle in his eyes and loved to arm wrestle with anyone who would challenge him, especially me.

Quickly, he learned to keep my attention by doing magic tricks, making things appear then disappear. He asked Oma to bake cookies, then he would hide them, knowing that I would spend hours looking for them like a drug junkie, desperate to get his fix. He was kind and gentle, and spoke his mind on all conflicts that the family faced, always resolving the issue with a positive outcome.

I thought that he would have been an ideal diplomat because he could bring about peace between the worst of enemies. Although he liked people, he liked animals better. He always said, "You can trust animals even more than your best friend."

While living in Poland as a young man, he had developed a talent for taking care of bees and loved them so much that he had even made a career as a bee keeper. He showed me how bees liked him and how they respected him. He never wore protective garments and they never attacked or stung him. He would say to me, "Bees are like good friends: if you treat them kindly and gently, they'll respond in kind."

I was awed by his strength and agility. He showed me how to swing an ax to chop wood.

At the end of the day, he would reward himself with a shot of schnapps, a ninety degree proof liquor that he would gulp down. I had tried schnapps once and I still remember the scalding sensation it left in my throat. Never again.

I grew fond of Opa, even allowing myself to chat in German, which was not easy for me.

We became the best of friends, and Mother learned to rely on him. He loved Oma and showed it in front of us by giving her an occasional pat on her behind or a quick peck on her lips. He had learned a few words of French that he used in his own style at supper time. "Quoi pour diner ce soir?" (What's for dinner tonight?)

Oma would shake her head. She could read lips in German, but not in French. So, she would turn to me for translation, and I would say, in my own style, "Was ist fur Abendessen?"

Oma was a dedicated cook and homemaker, and everyone loved her potato pancakes (latkes), cakes, pies, cookies, casseroles, and wiener schnitzels.

She was patient with others but not herself. Everything had to be perfect. Was there enough bread for everyone? Did we have warm clothing when we were out? Were the beds clean enough?

She spoke in a "funny way." Her speech was slurred and muffled, but after some getting used to it, I learned to make out the words. She had learned to cope with her deafness by reading lips, but only in German. I could tell if she understood what I was trying to say because she smiled and nodded at the same time, and it was a good feeling to know that I had reached her.

I was amazed to think of the terrible disruption they suffered in their sixth decade of life. They had spoken of all the Jewish friends they had left behind and how much they had feared for them. We never heard from them, even after the war, speculating that most had not survived and had become just another number in the statistics of the Holocaust.

Opa and Oma were safe. Or so they said. And so did my father and mother. And I was happy to have all these grown-ups shower me with love, care and warmth. We were going to be one big happy family, safe behind the big Maginot Line.

5- The Debacle

Two weeks after the war broke out my father was drafted and left for the army. He gave me a hug, waved goodbye and said, "Take good care of your mother. You are a big boy now."

He turned to Mother and said, "You'll be all right now that Opa and Oma are here with you."

He said one last thing, "I'll be back sooner than you think. The krauts will never be able to stand up to us. We are the French Army. They'll be sorry. Believe me."

He was so confident and reassuring that even Opa and Oma smiled and looked as if they had forgotten their horrendous escape from hell. I remember his loud laugh, and his singing the "Marseillaise" as he walked down the street, cocky and confident.

The house was empty without him, but Opa, Oma and Mother resumed a new routine, giving Opa an opportunity to fill in for the tasks father used to do. Life went on with a new rhythm, and for a while, I forgot that a war was on.

It was at least two months before we heard the first blasts from the German artillery firing a few kilometers away from across the Rhine.

Almost simultaneously, we heard the threatening drone and howling of stukas dotting the skies and, like vultures, they dove and released their bombs above our heads. A black smoke was smearing the skies above us, filling the air with an awful acid smell. Miraculously no one got hurt. In the neighborhood, I heard people say, 'Where is the French Air Force? Where is the DCA?' (Anti-aircraft guns) No one seemed to know.

Explosions were sounding closer and closer as the days went by. It was hard to sleep at night, listening to these thundering blasts in the distance and the wailing of the sirens announcing a new air raid.

Each night the loud booms of firing cannons was getting closer than the day before.

This was the beginning of my first nightmare, which became the topic of a recurring dream for years to come.

Mother must have gotten scared because she said, "We are leaving tonight. Get your things ready right now." I rushed upstairs and started packing my collection of toy soldiers.

"You won't be needing those, George. There are real soldiers out there," she said.

Having packed their little suitcase they had brought from Austria, Opa and Oma looked ready to leave right away. They agreed that there was no time to waste and they sighed with relief when they heard Mother make the announcement.

Mother didn't know how to drive the beautiful Hotchkiss that my father had bought the year before. So, she asked our chauffeur to drive us to Paris the next day. He was an old burly Alsatian who argued with Mother about her predictions of an enemy invasion. Judging from his slow response, bordering on resistance, it looked as if he didn't oppose the German policy of annexation. But Mother was insistent, and raising her voice, she said in her best Alsatian dialect, "Hans, you must drive us to Paris, you hear? I want you to do it right now. There is no time to waste."

He was not used to such direct orders, but yielded to Mother, who looked so adamant. Although he couldn't be trusted, we had no choice. We were totally dependent on him. All we could do was to expect that he would follow Mother's orders as he had done when my father was around.

He helped carry the heavy suitcases to the car and packed several baskets of food on the back seats.

The car was crammed with everything essential for our survival: bedding, suitcases full of clothes, towels, mementos and old photographs and my books by Jules Verne, Victor Hugo and Alexander Dumas.

"Why are we leaving at night?" I asked.

"We don't want the neighbors to know. People will talk and make trouble if they know."

I felt both excitement and dread. I was happy to leave my school and I would never have to see Mr. Himmler again. I would never have to face the stone-throwing kids in my neighborhood. On the other hand, I would miss my beautiful room, my electric train, my bookshelves full of my favored books, and my huge collection of toy lead soldiers.

We left at midnight. Mother sat in the front seat with Hans and I squeezed in between Opa and Oma in the back seat.

As the car was creeping through the thick night fog, the light beams were flooding the road ahead. The cool mist was like a white wall that was moving back slowly in front of us.

All around us there were people walking and pulling wheel carts full of suitcases and household effects in the middle of the road creating a traffic jam in the near total darkness. Beams of flashlights were lighting up the road ahead, as the fleeing hordes were trying to find their way among cars, bicycles, wheel carts, horse and buggies and hundreds of refugees.

"Who are all these people?" I asked.

"People who want to get away from the Germans" my mother whispered.

French troops, horse-driven cannons, tanks, armored trucks and supply trucks were going in the opposite direction towards the border.

We drove all night, through endless winding roads, while Opa and Oma were dozing off.

We arrived in Paris by morning and immediately proceeded to Uncle Dave and Aunt Ethel's apartment. We were exhausted, and were taken to a guest bedroom.

48

Hans decided to stay with an old acquaintance and said, "If you plan to stay in Paris, I should go back to Strasbourg tomorrow."

"No, Hans, We'll decide tomorrow what to do. So please, be here at eight o'clock in the morning," said my mother with a firm tone of voice.

He waved goodbye, but Mother admitted that she was not sure that he would return the next day. He had the keys to the car, and we were all at his mercy.

* * *

We awoke fresh, and ready to discuss the next phase of our getaway. We all sat in the living room, Uncle Dave, Aunt Ethel, Opa, Oma, Mother, Cousin Betty and me.

"How far do you think will be safe?" asked Mother.

"You have nothing to fear. Paris will be just fine," answered Uncle Dave.

"But what if the Germans reach Paris?" said Mother.

"That'll never happen. You are overreacting to the situation, Bertha," added Ethel.

"We would be so happy if you could all stay and we could all be together. Everything will be fine, and…"

Mother interrupted and said, "I just don't have a good feeling about all this. I would like to make sure."

"Well, then why don't you go as far as you can go," Ethel retorted.

"Yeah, and where would that be?" said mother, annoyed.

"Go to Bordeaux, Biarritz or Toulouse! But we think you're overdoing it," Ethel replied.

"Bordeaux does sound nice. It's near the coast. I heard it's a nice city," Mother said, "and no enemy has ever gotten close to that. Not since the Romans. Not since the Moors conquered Spain and France," she added half serious, half joking.

Uncle Dave countered, "Do you believe that Hans will agree to take you there?"

"Chances are, he'll resist. But I know how to convince him with a few hundred francs. He's never turned down the color of money," Mother said with a confident tone.

Opa and Oma, who had remained silent until then, not understanding the discussion in French, asked to be included in the discussion. After a quick translation into German, they approved of the Bordeaux destination.

We were going to the safest place in France: the Southwest, the farthest place from this ogre behind the Maginot Line, ready to pounce again.

All of a sudden, the war had become a reality. It no longer was a movie drama, a historical novel or a playground for toy soldiers and tanks.

It was right there, penetrating every aspect of our life, changing our ways, our home, our thoughts while igniting new fears and planting new doubts. On our trip across France, we had heard refugees say, "The French army will prevail. We'll be back soon. It's going to be like a short vacation." We heard others ask, 'How long do you think these Germans can last?'

But the real question was not how long they would last, but how many of us would still be alive at the end of the war?

6- Bordeaux

Uncle David, Aunt Ethel and Cousin Betty lived in an elegant district in Paris where Uncle David had his dental practice. They were convinced that it was premature to pack up and leave the city. They would wait and assess the war situation over the next few months. Mother, Opa, Oma and I, on the other hand, prepared to leave for Bordeaux as a final destination.

Hans showed up the next day in his overalls and work shoes, ready to turn over the car keys to Mother. But after a few rough exchanges, Mother prevailed when she said, "Hans, I'll give you five hundred francs, and you can keep the car and go back to Strasbourg." He took the money and looked relieved to be rid of us.

We arrived in Bordeaux by train on a dreary fall day, but were surprised to find mild temperatures after the rigorous winters we had endured in Alsace for all those years.

Bordeaux is a pleasant city on the river Garonne, leading to an estuary that empties into the Atlantic Ocean, about 50 miles from Bordeaux. I guess Mother had chosen this city because it was so distant from the front that the Germans would never get close to us. The war seemed so far away that it gave us a false sense of security. People in this city were friendly and very hopeful, so different from the people in Alsace, who were anti-French, anti-Semitic, unfriendly and glad to see us leave.

Before long Mother, Opa and Oma said they felt at home in this newly-adopted city. After we were settled in a new apartment, a new neighborhood, and a new school, life had become normal again.

While Mother looked into new business opportunities to make a living, Oma made a pleasant home for all of us, cooking wonderful meals, despite the severe rationing of bread, butter, milk, meat and eggs.

She decorated the apartment, put a touch of old Austria with her beautiful flowers and clean linen in every room and waited by the window at the end of the day, after having knitted sweaters for each of us and for my absent father.

She was always ready to hug and kiss when we came through the door. I loved her warm embrace and her gentle smile, as she handed me a piece of strudel she had baked that day.

We missed my father who was fighting on the German front somewhere in the East. We waited for several months, for a letter but none had come. Finally we stopped waiting, keeping thoughts to ourselves and wondering what might be the reason for the silence.

We didn't talk about the worst possible outcome, but couldn't bring ourselves to mention any positive ones either. Mother would say that there was no point in speculating because it was a waste of time. But I asked myself: Was he captured by the Germans? Or was he hiding somewhere in the wilderness? Or was he dead? Newsreels gave little clues because they were mostly focused on propaganda.

I started a new set of nightmares. *Papa is in the trenches at the front. He is throwing grenades. Suddenly, he screams as an artillery shell explodes near him. He collapses in a river of blood that fills the trenches and disappears under the surface. His hands reach out, pointing to the sky.*

I'd wake up, crying out his name hysterically, "Papa, Papa, Papa!"

Seconds later, Mother would rush into my bedroom, saying,

"What's the matter, George. Are you're having a bad dream?"

She'd comfort me, as we'd talk about the dream. "You know, Papa will be back. He is very strong and very clever. You'll see." And reassured, I'd go back to sleep, hoping for a quieter dream.

*   *   *

Like most French cities, Bordeaux had become a target for the German Luftwaffe. The Germans had planned to spread fear in the population by making unpredictable air raids and by bombing civilian dwellings and shopping areas. Their purpose was to demoralize the population and force the country to surrender.

German planes did not target military installations. They unloaded their bombs at random in the center of cities. No one was safe. Shelters were still lacking, and people didn't know where to go for safety. Some took refuge in their own cellar, if one existed in their house or to neighborhood shelters.

Air raids occurred at any time and there were no warnings or discernible patterns. Wailing sirens would go off day or night, whether one was at lunch, dinner, on the toilet, in the shower or in bed.

My worst fear was that bombs would start falling while I was still on the toilet with no time to finish my business. I think it probably changed my bathroom habits for years and I had to make sure, like my two cats, that I always had an escape route.

*   *   *

Four months after we had moved into our apartment, the sirens woke us up in the middle of the night. It was the night of May 20, 1940.

We got up, threw a bathrobe over our pajamas and prepared to go into the cellar, which was our usual routine. Oma would have to be told about the air raid because she couldn't hear the sirens and the planes overhead. This usually took extra time, and delayed the family's exodus down the stairs and into the cellar several flights below.

Other people in the building preferred to line up in front of the elevator and the door leading to the cellar.

While we were getting Oma ready, taking warm blankets and slippers, we heard a bomb whistling through the air. The sound was deafening and terrifying. Seconds later, it exploded close by, probably on the next building. We heard people shrieking.

Mother yelled, "It's the next house! My God! What are they doing?"

The blast was so powerful and loud that Oma had heard it. Frightened, she fell to the floor. Mother and Opa rushed to help her up, but she lay there unconscious and lifeless.

In the moonlight shining through the window, my mother screamed, "Oh, my God. She is dead! She is dead! Oh, my God!" I stood there, in the corner of the room, frozen, unable to move or say anything.

Mother couldn't stop moaning and wailing and Opa broke into sobs. Explosions and blasts continued around us, but no one seemed to care anymore. I didn't know what to do. A strange acid smell was filling the air, and the crashing noise all around was frightening. My eyes were full of bits of plaster from the ceiling. Outside the window, I could see flashing lights from anti-aircraft guns alternating with exploding bombs.

We huddled together in the dark—Opa, mother and I— holding each other tightly and squeezing Oma's lifeless body, while deafening and thunderous explosions continued around us.

The next day thick black smoke enveloped the city. Mother and I walked in a daze, confused, defeated, looking for friends and neighbors in buildings reduced to rubble. Where would help come from? What to do about poor Oma?

We came back to the apartment. Opa was collapsed over Oma's body, unable to leave her.

"Opa, we'll take care of the details," Mother said, "We'll take good care of her. Please, let her go."

Opa's face was taut and drawn. He stayed on his knees, holding his head between his fists, sobbing, "My Oma. My dear Oma. Why? Why? Why?" Bending over her body, he was beating his fists on the parquet floor.

Watching this strange spectacle, I was overcome by intense fear and sadness mixed with a boiling rage. War had come so close to home, and this ugly but faceless enemy had come right into our living room to spread panic, doom and death.

My brain was on fire. My thoughts were zigzagging. My muscles were tight. My fists and teeth were clenched.

Who would be the next victim? Father, Mother, Opa, or I?

Oma's funeral was the saddest thing I had ever experienced. It was heart-breaking to see Opa with stooped shoulders, shuffling along to the grave site. He had not eaten for days and looked haggard and worn-out. Mother couldn't stop from sobbing and held on to Opa's arm as they walked to her tomb. I followed alone ten steps behind them, wondering how many more times I would have to walk to a cemetery during this war.

Years later I still get teary-eyed when I recount Oma's story.

7- Petain and De Gaulle

The war lasted seventeen days! German troops had made their attack in May 1940, pouring several divisions of well-trained soldiers and Panzer divisions into the Netherlands, Belgium and Northern France, advancing through the Ardennes.

The French had good firepower with heavier artillery (horse-drawn, as did the Germans) and good tanks, but basically relied on their stationary defenses, the Maginot Line, to stop the enemy.

Germans were more mobile and used a blitzkrieg strategy, utilizing tanks supported by tactical air power that caught the French and Allied troops by surprise.

The result was a total debacle in which the Belgian and French Army were severed and encircled. Most remaining divisions became totally ineffective because supply arteries were cut off by air attacks.

The defeat occurred despite the fact that both sides had roughly the same number of fighting troops (two and a half million men).

Fierce Panzer divisions made their way through the Ardennes Forest, which the French thought was impenetrable and had barely defended.

In the North fleeing troops tried desperately to reach Dunkirk, where thousands were killed before they could board ships to England.

In the South, the French fought bravely, but were clearly overpowered, outmaneuvered and defeated.

From May 10th on, the war was moving at a fast pace. Germans were advancing at record speed in all directions. There was no time to regroup or reorganize.

The Netherlands collapsed on May 14th and Belgium surrendered on May 28th. From March to June 1940, military and governmental organizations were crumbling everywhere.

There was chaos, confusion, morale decay, uncertainty, corruption, disbelief and gloom. Officials walked around as if they were drunk, drugged or utterly depressed. Military commanders looked as though they were fighting windmills without the slightest notion where the enemy was going to strike. Furthermore, the French army had the wrong kind of tanks. Most were designed to support the infantry, not the lightning warfare which Charles de Gaulle had advocated and which the Germans had adopted so effectively. In addition the army was hindered by an obsolete system of communication

The war was called a "phony war." It wasn't really a war. It was a surprise raid by mobile armored units, a war strategy which became known as "blitzkrieg" (lightning war) and was perfected since WWI. Hitler coined the word "Blitzkrieg" in a speech at the 1935 Nuremberg Party Rally which went unnoticed by the rest of Europe.

After May, German troops advanced at a bewildering pace.

On June 5th, to the surprise of the military and the civilian population, the German army and Panzer divisions headed towards Paris. Four days later, the German General (General Bock) drove his forces below Paris.

By the 14th of June, the Wehrmacht had entered Paris! Millions of panic-stricken French men, women and children had fled southwards.

On June 22nd, the French forces surrendered, after having been trapped in their own territory behind the Maginot Line.

"No one who lived through the French debacle of May-June 1940 ever quite got over the shock," said historian Robert O. Paxton. "For Frenchmen, confident of a special role in the world, the six weeks' defeat by German armies was a shattering trauma."

*　　*　　*

Diplomatic developments were moving along just as fast as military developments.

On the 25th of June, the Germans granted an armistice to Marshal Petain, who had gotten the approval of General Weygand. Under the terms of the armistice, France would be divided into occupied and non-occupied zones. The *zone occupee*, which included the northern three-fifth of France as well as a strip of land running down the Atlantic coast to the Spanish border, contained most of France's industrial wealth and population. The *zone libre* (unoccupied zone), was the poorest part of France. Separating the zones was the Demarcation Line, a internal military border, which the Germans could open or close as they wished.

This line would become so strictly adhered to that even French government officials would not freely cross it. It functioned like a sealed border, and anyone caught crossing the border would get shot. Millions of refugees who had fled the invasion were prevented from crossing it. Complaints about lack of food and other problems could be blamed on Petain's government rather than the Germans since Petain was forced to care for the refugees for two to three months. This was a calculated move by the Germans, because it gave them enough time to appear organized and generous while they established an efficient occupation in the north.

On June 29 the Petain's government was moved to Vichy, the world-renowned health spa town on the northern edge of the Auvergne, in the heart of Bourbon country, noted for its sparkling water (Perrier water).

General Heinrich von Stulpnagel was named the commander of all territories in occupied France including Bordeaux.

(Incidentally, he did distinguish himself later on, when he conspired in a plot to assassinate Hitler in July 1944. Unfortunately, he was caught and was executed.)

The Franco-German armistice, approved by both sides, was signed by Marshal Petain, whose heroism during the First World War still inspired popular confidence. The armistice split the country in two: the Alsace and Moselle regions were annexed by Germany, the North was occupied by the German army, and the South was to be governed from the city of Vichy, under the leadership of Marshal Philippe Petain.

The newly formed French government—initially formed in Bordeaux— moved to Vichy. It was still in command of roughly 100,000 troops, which were disbanded two years later.

Marshal Philippe Petain and his Prime Minister, Pierre Laval, became known as "the collaborators" which became synonymous with "traitors" to the Free French of Charles de Gaulle.

Laval turned out to be an ideal scapegoat for Petain. He was an evil man and stopped at nothing for power and money. Half the French population hated him. But both Petain and Laval were hoping to gain public acceptance in exchange for a return to a normal and orderly life in France. Hitler had offered the armistice to France, expecting that it would bring him economic advantages. Immediately after the armistice was signed, the new French government settled in Vichy, a small city in central France on the Allier river. The city has been renowned since Roman times for its famous Vichy spring water which is exported all over the world.

While the Germans were making themselves at home in France, Hitler continued the pursuit of his wild dreams. Next stop, in his mind, was England.

In July 1940, the Germans began bombing England. The question on everybody's mind was: Would England be able to stand up against this formidable power, ready to conquer all of Europe in one clean sweep?

I remember how Mother cheered after listening to Churchill's speech on the BBC in June 1940, a few days before the final fall of France. Churchill's cavernous and authoritative voice warmed our hearts, as we listened to the radio. To a cheering Parliament, he said.

"We shall not flag or fall. We shall go on to the end; we shall fight in France; we shall fight on the seas and oceans; we shall fight with growing confidence and growing strength in the air; we shall defend our island, whatever the cost may be; we shall fight on the beaches;

we shall fight on the landing grounds; we shall fight in the fields and in the streets; we shall fight in the hills; we shall never surrender, and even if, which I do not for a moment believe, this island or a large part of it were subjugated and starving, then our Empire beyond the seas, armed and guarded by the British Fleet, would carry on the struggle, until, in God's good time, the New World, with all its power and might, steps forth to the rescue and liberation of the Old."

What a moment in history! What a soothing and hopeful message—words that were going to sustain our morale for months and years to come!

When I heard on the radio that French prisoners would be treated according to the Geneva convention, I began to hope that Father was one of the prisoners, still alive and well enough to survive the ordeal.

* * *

We listened to the radio morning and evening, then discussed the bulletins that were making history day by day, hoping that we would pick up more news about French POWs and get a clue about Father's whereabouts. But the radio remained silent on that topic.

France was in shambles, still reeling from the shock of the defeat.

No one could understand how the strongest army in Europe could be defeated so quickly and easily. The losses in this seventeen day war had been staggering—90,000 dead, 200,000 wounded, more than one million taken prisoner.

The French Government was in total disarray. Edouard Daladier, the radical Socialist Premier who had been in power since 1938, had followed Neville Chamberlain's policy of appeasement with Hitler. He, too, had signed the Munich Agreement, which gave the Sudetenland of Czechoslovakia to Germany. Daladier resigned in March 1940. He was interned by the Vichy government and tried in February 1942 for "betraying his country." After his trial, he was deported to Germany and held there until the end of the war, when he successfully returned to French politics.

After Daladier's resignation, Paul Reynaud became Premier on March 21st. He was a strong advocate of resistance against the German Western Offensive launched in May 1940. He supported

Churchill's proposal for an Anglo-French Union but had failed to get support and was forced to resign by Petain on June 16, 1940. Petain, the eighty-four-year-old Marshal, the "hero of Verdun," took over and formed a new government. The next day he addressed the people of France in a radio message, "With a heavy heart, I tell you that it is necessary to end the fighting." He said that he would sign an armistice with Germany, believing that Britain would not survive a German attack and that by signing a peace treaty with Berlin, France would emerge from defeat stronger and more united than ever in a new Europe dominated by Germany.

Petain's assurances soothed ninety-five percent of the public, and he was hailed as a male Joan of Arc, "the leader who saved us from the abyss." But he had expressed just what the people wanted to hear. Most were relieved that they had been spared from chaos and an all-out war. To cushion the blow of defeat, Petain argued that under the Third Republic the people of France "had been honestly led into war but dishonestly led into defeat."

Even after support for the Vichy government started to fade, faith in Petain remained high. For most French, there was a clear distinction between Vichy on the one hand and Petain on the other. Crowds adored him and the Church worshipped him: *"La France, c'est Petain, et Petain, c'est la France,"* said the French Cardinal Gelier. On the road crowds of men and women lined the rails when his train passed by.

In those first six months after the new government came into power people believed that Petain, a benevolent grandfather figure who professed to want what was best for France was just what the country needed. Under the slogan "Travail, Famille, Patrie" ("Work, Family, Fatherland"), Vichy set out to rejuvenate France by promoting youth organizations., the pursuit of sports and a healthier outdoor lifestyle. It also encouraged a greater role for the Catholic Church in education.

But there was a darker side to the Vichy government. Despite the values of Liberty, Equality and Fraternity, married women were prevented from holding jobs: their real job was to stay home and have children.

For others it was much worse. Within two months of coming to power Vichy published a series of decrees making Jews second-class citizens. Immigrant Jews were stripped of their rights, constantly harassed and threatened with deportation. "France for the French," said the Vichy politicians. Communists and Freemasons were hunted down. Trade unions were abolished. All elected officials were replaced by pro-Vichy nominees.

A lot of finger-pointing followed. No one admitted responsibility and everyone blamed someone else. Ordinary soldiers blamed their officers. Generals blamed politicians. Politicians of the Right blamed politicians of the Left. and vice versa. Most people blamed the Communists. The Communists blamed the Fascists, and the Fascists blamed the Jews.

In September, Reynaud was arrested by Petain's Vichy government and he, too, like Daladier, was tried in the notorious Riom Trial in 1942, a trial which had been put on to show the Germans the good will of the French.

*   *   *

The armistice was signed on June 25th, 1940, and de Gaulle had already fled to London on June 17th.

The following day De Gaulle broadcast a dramatic appeal to his countrymen over the BBC, which Prime Minister Winston Churchill had put at his disposal.

Again, we put our ears close to the radio speakers, trying to catch every word De Gaulle was uttering. We did not say a word while he was speaking for fear of missing something. At times, we did miss some of his words that were drowned in the static.

He told the French people that they had lost a battle, but not the war. He was confident of Britain's ability to continue the war and was hopeful that the United States would not only provide more economic help, but might get involved with fighting troops.

He urged Frenchmen to join him in London, fight for Free France and keep alive what he called 'the flame of French resistance.'

I asked Mother, "How can we join him? I want to go with him."

"You're not old enough, George. But some day, who knows?" she replied as she smiled at me.

George M. Burnell, M.D.

The appeal was not a great success. By the end of July, only 7,000 volunteers had joined Free France. De Gaulle was declared a traitor by the Vichy government. Churchill countered by officially recognizing de Gaulle as the leader of the Free France movement.

As the new French leader, de Gaulle could recruit fighting men and continue his BBC broadcasts.

De Gaulle consolidated his position in Africa, and with the help of British equipment, Free French troops began to engage in small-scale military operations in Central Africa, Egypt, Eritrea and Syria. In these localities de Gaulle's forces captured 25,000 Vichy troops.

The Free French forces were just a token force among the Allies. Having started with only 7,000 volunteers, they grew to 230,000 men, all stationed in Algiers.

*   *   *

Each night we ran down to the cellar to listen to the latest developments on the BBC. It was a modest beginning but it gave people enough hope to maintain their morale.

I asked Mother, "How long will this war last?" She looked at me as if I had asked the most critical question of all times and said, "Long enough for all of us to remember it the rest of our lives."

"What about my friend Hans?" I asked.

"I called his family the other day to inquire about our property. Hans's mother said that it was confiscated and that a German family had moved in. She also said that all the signs were changed into German. No one was allowed to speak French. His mother said that even if you say *bonjour*, you could be sent to a concentration camp," Mother said.

"What is Hans going to do?"

"He will have to join the Hitler Youth if he wants to go on to high school. His two older brothers will have to volunteer in the German army. The parents will have to join the Nazi Party. If they refuse, his family will be sent to a camp," said Mother.

"Is there anything we can do?" I asked.

"I'm afraid not."

I was sad and felt helpless. I wanted to scream but couldn't utter a word.

8- Wistiti

Bordeaux was in the midst of a dramatic change. It had been a port city of 250,000 for decades, but now with hordes of refugees fleeing the German invasion, it was crammed with nearly a million. There were gun emplacements and flags with Nazi insignias draped everywhere. The port itself, a shipping point for Bordeaux wine producers for more than two hundred years was now teeming with armed soldiers and being converted into a German naval base.

It was very difficult seeing German soldiers marching up and down our streets. The German army in their green uniform, the Wehrmacht as they were called, seemed at ease in our shops, restaurants, cafes and markets.

They wore heavy black boots and loved to clack their heels while shouting a loud "Heil Hitler", pointing their right arm towards the sky, often followed by "Deutchland Uber Alles". The tune of "Lily Marlene" was blaring in the streets and the city parks.

Mother was reluctant to let me go out on the street by myself. There were rumors that the German Police were rounding up Jews,

Communists or French resistance fighters. People were reporting "suspicious neighbors" to the authorities, and we didn't know whom to trust, because our friends might be the very ones who would betray us. Rewards for reporting or ransom money was to be given for all those who had valuable information for the authorities. People were afraid to hide Jews because they knew too well that Germans had set up a transit camp at Merignac on the edge of Bordeaux and that trains packed with Jews of all ages and nationalities were running out of the Gare St. Jean directly to Auschwitz.

Like everyone else Mother and Grandfather wondered how life would change in Bordeaux. They were relieved when Marshal Petain took over as head of state and comforted by his grandfatherly assurances that he would protect all French citizens against the worst excesses of the Germans. Their feelings changed, however, when they saw Bordeaux's 5,000 Jews being forced to wear yellow Stars of David. They were further dismayed when Petain's government stripped immigrant and refugee Jews of their rights and property and began deporting them.

George M. Burnell, M.D.

We worried about the Marcuses and the Abramses who we knew were in hiding and we were afraid to contact them for fear of being traced and followed.

Before I went out to see friends Mother would say, "Be careful what you say to your friends or strangers. Don't talk about politics, religion, or the Germans. You never know which one might be a collaborator."

French Jews were required to register at the Police station and wear a yellow Star of David, although the enforcement for wearing the star was not strictly enforced. Mother decided that it would be more prudent for her to wear a gold cross on a beautiful gold chain around her neck. The one inch cross was displayed so that no one could miss seeing it. It was like flashing a passport with "Non-Jew" stamped on it.

Mother never forgot to wear her cross, which became as crucial for her as a bullet proof vest in a shooting rampage. I never wore a cross myself, but did learn how to cross myself whenever people seemed to doubt my faith or question my religious affiliation.

*   *   *

After one year in the apartment, we moved to the harbor where mother bought a full bar and restaurant, catering to French, German and Italian sailors. I thought that it was daring on her part, but she said that it would be easier to hide among the enemy troops than among French civilians.

The restaurant was on a major street, a few blocs from the piers where all the big merchant marine ships, oilers, tankers, and war ships were anchored.

It was exciting to snoop around the docks and watch the unloading of huge crates, trucks, military materiel, machinery, and large containers of food. When I got too close to the "No entry" sign, an armed guard would wave me on and say, "Don't get closer or I'll shoot." That was convincing enough for me to back off. I'd return to the restaurant, hoping that the next day, a new sentry would be more civil and understanding of my curiosity.

One day a French sailor whose ship had just sailed in from North Africa, brought in a cute little monkey and asked Mother, "Would you like to have him?"

I could sense her hesitation. During this crucial moment the monkey's eyes and mine became locked in a fixed gaze, and I said, "Please, Mother, let's get him."

"No, George. We can't afford to have a monkey in the house."

"I swear I'll take care of him. I promise. I promise. Please, please..."

She gave in and asked the sailor, "How much do you want for him?"

"Just give me enough to drink and eat this week while I am in port, and we'll call it even," the sailor said, winking at me.

Mother looked at me, watching for my reaction, and seeing my pleading eyes, accepted the offer. The sailor took the little monkey off his shoulder and put him down on the counter.

I was so happy. I couldn't sit still. The little monkey might have sensed it because he jumped into my lap, and with his tiny hands grasped my fingers. I lifted him to my chest, and he put his arms around my neck, looking back at his former master, the sailor. I thought "He must not have had a strong bonding with the sailor, who seemed relieved to be rid of him."

"What's his name?" I asked the sailor.

"Wistiti. That's what we call him."

Wistiti was as big as a cuddly teddy bear. He had long slim furry arms with cute little hands big enough to hold a liquor glass, and beady dark eyes with a gaze that fixed straight into my eyes. His furless bottom seemed odd to me, but in time, I would get used to it. I'd get him a pair of tailored short pants.

He had complete control of the tail that he used for a variety of balancing acts, including hanging from the counter railing with his head down, rolling his round eyes to see the reactions on people's faces. Then, he would open his mouth and make a shrilling high pitch sound, which was his way of asking for a reward of peanuts or a banana.

Wistiti and I became good friends from the beginning. We became inseparable. I couldn't wait to come home from school every day, knowing that he was waiting for me at the door.

Wistiti became the darling of the house. In the evening, while drinking at the bar, German, Italian, French sailors and dock workers loved to buy drinks for Wistiti. They discovered that his favored drinks included creme of cocoa, creme de menthe, Benedictine and anisette, although he never refused a good cognac. Using both of his tiny hands, Wistiti would grab his drink in a small liquor glass, raise it to this little mouth and gulp the content down. Sailors would clap, laugh and sing along and yell "One more round for the little one."

After a half dozen drinks, Wistiti would act like a drunken sailor, weaving between the tables and throwing liquor glasses on the floor. I was afraid that he would get sick, and I wanted to take him away from this rowdy crowd, but I was unable to exert my authority against such overwhelming military pressure from all the foreign navies.

Mother was delighted to see that Wistiti was as much of an attraction for all the men as the beautiful waitresses were and she congratulated me for having insisted on adopting little Wistiti. It was turning out to be good business and he was earning his keep. But I was afraid that he was turning into an alcoholic. No one else seemed to care, and I was worried sick.

I shared my worries with Mother, but she pleaded with me to let Wistiti "have a good time at happy hour."

Poor Wistiti was entertaining the troops all right, but he was being used and would eventually pay a high price with his alcoholism. His hangovers were awful. He would throw up, retch and make shrilling sounds that would pierce my heart. I began to dread the cocktail hour and tried to find closets where I could hide little Wistiti. But customers, wondering where the little monkey was hiding, would pressure Mother to find him. She would beg me to bring him out, and the whole drunken routine would start all over. I'd give Wistiti pep talks, urging him to stop drinking, but he wouldn't listen. He was hooked, and there was nothing I could do to stop this awful spectacle each evening.

* * *

Mother employed several beautiful young waitresses who tended to the sailors in the bar and in the restaurant. Although they competed for the customers' attention, they forgave Wistiti for his popularity and they adopted him like a teacher's pet.

After reporting to work, they would go upstairs on the second floor above the restaurant to undress and change into their uniform. It was a large room with several full size mirrors and comfortable sofas and chairs in front of vanity counters where they could put on their cosmetics and freshen up.

Wistiti soon discovered the dressing room and asked to be admitted and he gained admission to the girls' private quarters.

As we were inseparable, I had made my entrance with him, and to my delight, I too had been accepted without any resistance. After all, I was just a boy, and my presence was no threat to the girls.

They would reveal their beautiful bodies in skimpy lingerie while putting on their nylon black stockings and high heel shoes. They seemed totally uninhibited in front of me and Wistiti and walked around topless and sometimes bottomless, much to my delight. They provided me with many wonderful dreams and fantasies, satisfied all my voyeuristic desires, and helped me cope with my emerging and raging hormones.

My favored waitress was Nicole, a slender, gorgeous girl with long blond hair, blue eyes, thin legs, beautiful white skin, and a charming angelic smile. She often said to me in her tiny cute voice, "I like the way you look at me, George. If you were a little older, I would fall in love with you and marry you."

It was excruciatingly painful for me to hear this declaration from Nicole with my adolescent hormones simmering and leaving me with a tremendous urge to get relief from the growing tumescence in my trousers. Wistiti, too, seemed to get excited, his red penis sticking out like a lipstick.

I wasn't sure that the basis for his stimulation was the same as mine, although the girls noticed his red swollen penis with great interest and amusement.

I started having recurring dreams of Nicole and I, making love to her in the garden, in the swimming pool, on the beach, and even in the warmth of my bed. What delicious dreams! I always felt wonderful in the morning, even though I knew I couldn't have Nicole to myself—not till I grew older.

I was just happy that Wistiti had provided me with this voyeuristic outlet and I never complained despite the aching turgidity that plagued me every day. Sometimes, relief came through what I later learned were referred to as "wet dreams", and I was thankful for the temporary release.

However, these good times with Wistiti were not to last. A huge problem arose.

Wistiti loved to get attention, and after a few drinks, he was the life of the party at the bar. He knew how to roll his dark, scintillating eyes, make pirouettes on the bar counter and win everybody's heart. Customers would pull out their chairs into a circle in the the bar, giving him center stage, which he loved.

Once in the circle, he would bow, make somersaults, pull on mens' trousers, beg for another drink by gesticulating and pretending to drink with his thumb. Everyone would laugh and no one could resist buying him another drink.

The waitresses dreaded the new routine, because Wistiti would jump from the bar to the floor, insist on looking up their dress, and climb up their legs, causing irreparable snags in their precious nylon stockings.

All the waitresses: Nicole, Francoise, Veronique, Fifi, and Sandrine became furious. After weeks of this intolerable situation, they asked Mother to pay for their torn nylon stockings and caused a huge conflict between them and Mother, who refused to buy them new stockings.

I wanted to buy the stockings but didn't have the money. Nylons were particularly expensive, as they were available only on the black market. German soldiers often handed them out to girls in exchange for promised dates (and sex I imagined).

Wistiti was a big drawing card for business, but there was a big price to pay. The waitresses no longer allowed him— and me—to come into their dressing room, while they changed into their uniforms, thus depriving me of my main sexual outlet.

Wistiti was losing favor with all of us, my mother, the waitresses, and now me. Now, it was he who was demanding to attend the cocktail hour, and it was he who was throwing a temper tantrum when we showed the slightest opposition.

But it was I, who had to take care of his hangovers! I felt that something had to give. I could no longer tolerate this unworkable situation. My mother was exasperated. The waitresses were threatening to quit. I felt helpless and didn't know where to turn for help.

One day, a German navy officer came in and asked Mother if he could have Wistiti to bring home to Germany. I listened to the conversation and became increasingly anxious as the exchanges between Mother and the officer heated up. After his request, Mother replied, "I don't think so. My son is so attached to him, he wouldn't allow it."

But the officer didn't give up and retorted in his harsh, grating and loud broken French:

"Madam, you don't understand. I want that monkey and I'll have it. I don't care what your son says. This monkey is going back to Germany with me. That's final."

"But I can't let you have it," retorted Mother.

The German officer was getting red in the face, and the tone of his voice was rising a couple octaves. He stopped speaking French and in his harsh German, he said:

"Sie sind verruckt, meine Dame (you are crazy, lady). Ich kann Ihnen viele Schwierigkeiten machen." (I can make lots of trouble for you.)

Mother looked scared. Her cross didn't seem to carry the magical power it was supposed to have in the face of such an overt threat. I wondered if this man had some suspicious information about our background. Did he know something that would put us in jeopardy? Had one of the waitresses complained to the authorities? This was no ordinary sailor. He was a high ranking officer, judging from all the insignia on his uniform.

At any rate, it didn't seem wise to cause any further commotion by provoking this man, who seemed implacable, and I nodded with Mother.

"All right, you can have him," said Mother in a voice that almost choked.

She asked me to hand over Wistiti to the German, who grasped him firmly with both arms. Wistiti looked as if he knew what was going on and started shrieking. Like a father whose child had been ripped away from him, I felt like my heart had been torn apart and I struggled to hold my tears and keep from striking the officer.

Mother looked at me with pleading eyes as if to say 'Please, be strong. Keep calm. Don't make any trouble.'

The officer smiled and said, "You're doing the right thing, and the Fuehrer would be proud of you. Heil Hitler," while clacking his heels and throwing his right arm high up in front of him.

Then he walked out with Wistiti who was looking at me and wailing desperately, being held against his will.

I felt helpless, devastated and heart-broken. Inside, I was boiling with rage against the German who had taken away my friend, my companion, my re-incarnated brother, my soul mate.

I plunged into grief and for days I could not eat, study or concentrate. Although it had solved their stocking problem, the waitresses felt sorry for me and offered support. They even let me come back to their private quarters upstairs where, during the change into their uniforms, the sight of their nude bodies eased my grief.

Later, I thought "Like my father, my Wistiti was going to be a POW in Germany! Would I ever see him again?"

9- Nicole

Two weeks later I was still grieving the loss of Wistiti and one Sunday morning, a momentous event took my mind off this terrible loss.

Mother was working in the kitchen and I was getting up, in my room.

"Guess who is here?" my mother yelled at the top of her voice.

Still sleepy, I muttered, "Who is it?"

"Quick. Quick. Come down and see for yourself. Hurry up!"

I jumped out of bed, rushed down the stairs in my pajamas, and still rubbing my eyes, I couldn't believe what I saw. Standing in the doorway was this tall, dark-haired, thin man, unshaven, dressed in rags, with deep sunken eyes

"Papa, Papa, it's Papa," I shouted while bolting into his arms.

"George. George. I'm back. I'm back. And I'm here to stay. For good. No kidding."

"I'm so happy, so happy," I kept saying while hugging and kissing him as I rode piggyback on his shoulders into the house.

He walked, bent over, and put me down before we got to the staircase. His voice sounded tired and remote like a man who had been up for days or weeks without sleep, food, or shelter. His feet had sores that were bleeding; his spindly legs looked bird-like; his hairy chest, visible through his torn shirt, showed a bony rib cage; his rabbi-like beard hung under a gaunt face where tired-looking eyes displayed a haggard gaze. Was that the robust, cocksure, happy father who had left our house the year before, singing the "Marseillaise" as he had waved us goodbye?

Mother hugged and kissed him while Opa watched with tears in his eyes. I kept hugging him. I couldn't believe he was real.

After the cascade of emotions subsided, he asked. "Any chance for a good bath, a change of clothes, a little soup and a warm bed?" We took him upstairs and waited on him hand and foot. After a bath, a shave and new clothes, he no longer looked like a homeless beggar, and I recognize the old smile and twinkle in his eyes.

"We must let Father rest," said Mother after she had warmed up some food that he devoured like a starved animal, gulping his soup and taking huge mouthfuls of the chicken sandwich Mother had prepared for him.

The rest of the day went by quickly, and my grief over Wistiti became less acute with the arrival of my father. All this emotion was a lot to absorb in two weeks, I thought.

We couldn't wait to hear Father's story, and how he got back from the front line, but we waited until the next day when he had gotten enough rest.

Father was ecstatic at finding us safe and sound. The restaurant was doing well, but he was irritated at knowing that Germans were part of the clientele.

"They spend good money and never argue over the check," said Mother, "and we are safe from the French police. They wouldn't dare look for trouble here."

After a brief family conference, we all agreed that Father should remain as invisible as a fly on the wall. To the waitresses, the neighbors and the delivery people, we would say that he was just another handyman that Mother had hired to do work around the house.

*   *   *

German soldiers were fond of our bar and restaurant. They loved the warm and accepting atmosphere with good food, good music and beautiful and receptive girls—especially Nicole, Fifi, Janine and Sandrine—to dance with to the tunes from our phonograph.

I didn't understand the rules of war. Was it a rule that victorious armies could take advantage of the beautiful girls of the conquered? Were girls supposed to entertain the victors? Was it their duty to do so? Would they later be considered collaborators with the enemy? Would they be judged as traitors or would they be prosecuted as spies? After all, Mother was nice to the Germans, and she wasn't a collaborator or a spy. Were the girls being nice just to divert the enemy's attention? I wasn't clear on whose side they were on, but I concluded that in war the sides often got blurred.

The soldiers were generous, and the girls looked like they were able to accommodate their desires. After closing time, the girls would leave arm in arm with the last soldiers, who had waited for them at the bar.

I wondered what the waitresses did on their own time. Did they go to another bar? Did they go home with the soldiers? Deep down, I bristled every time I would see "my Nicole" leave with one of the soldiers.

One day a terrible thing happened. I heard Mother scream in the kitchen. I came running down the stairs, my heart racing and my eardrums pounding, sensing that something awful had happened. Had she cut her finger again, as she had done a few months before? Or did she see a rat racing across the kitchen floor? When I got down, I saw Fifi, another of my favorite waitresses, in tears, talking to Mother. I hadn't caught the drift of the conversation when I got there, but I heard Mother shout, "Oh, non! Non! Non! C'est pas vrai! C'est pas possible! (It's not true. It's not possible).

"Qu'est-ce qui se passe?"(What's happening?) I asked nervously.

"C'est terrible, George," said mother, sobbing.

"Quoi. Quoi. Dis-moi!" (What, what, tell me), I yelled, sensing that I too would get upset.

Fifi, bawling uncontrollably, turned to me and said. "Nicole. It's Nicole."

"What about Nicole?" I yelled.

"Nicole is dead. She is dead. You hear. She was killed las night," Fifi said between sobs.

Cries and whimpers filled the air of the kitchen. Father, no longer restraining himself, had come out of the hallway where he had been hiding, to join the wailing group around the kitchen table.

I was stupefied. How could this be? My Nicole? My dear Nicole! My precious Nicole!

I didn't believe it. That was a lie. It was a bad joke. Or a bad dream? I felt as if I was about to pass out. I regained my senses and started asking questions. So many questions needed to be answered.

"What happened? How did it happen? Who was involved?"

We were all waiting for answers. Fifi was surrounded by the other girls: Sandrine, Veronique, Janine, Ginette, Marie, and Simone, who had heard the news and had come to the restaurant to hear explanations and to give support to Mother.

Mother was in shock. She was pale, paralyzed and unable to speak.

Fifi, still sobbing, finished the story.

"We were going home with these two hansome young soldiers," she said as she caught her breath. "They were so correct and polite, real gentlemen. Then, we were at Nicole's place." Again, Fifi stopped, gulping more air, and went on. "She and her escort said good night, and I left with the other fellow."

"You did that?" said Marie.

"Nicole was to call me in the morning, as she usually does."

"And then?" interrupted Sandrine.

"She never called. I became worried and went to her apartment," said Fifi, wiping her tears with the back of her hand, and went on.

"The concierge became suspicious, when she didn't see Nicole in the morning. She called the police. When they got no answer, they forced the door."

Fifi covered her eyes, as if she was blocking images from her mind. She went on. "And there she was, on the bed, naked, strangled, dead."

Fifi stopped, her body jerking with spasms, her voice crackling. Girls were crying and Mother was frozen. Father stood there unnoticed by the girls, his face grimacing with pain.

I was numb all over. I couldn't move. Another horrible death. First, Grandma, now Nicole. Who would be next? How much more can I take of this avalanche of bad news?

The investigation revealed that there had been a struggle in the apartment and screams had been heard, but the neighbors had not wanted to intervene, knowing that a German soldier was involved, "It would not have been safe to do so." They said it probably had been a lover's quarrel.

My mind was bursting with painful thoughts. She is dead! My beautiful Nicole whom I secretly loved and who said she would have married me if I had been older. How I wish I had been there to protect her and to save her. What a calamity!

I was crestfallen and couldn't concentrate. I missed several days of school. Mother and Father didn't put any pressure on me. They, too, were grieving and had closed the restaurant for the rest of the week.

More nightmares followed in which I saw myself single-handedly battling a squad of German soldiers who had put all the waitresses in a pit, threatening to burn them alive. As soldiers were shooting at me, suddenly I'd wake up, totally drenched with sweat.

During the day, I would ruminate incessantly. First, losing Grandma. Then Wistiti. Now Nicole. The three most important beings in my life after Mother and Father. That was too much, I thought. I would retreat to my room, sobbing for hours.

War was too cruel. Nothing made any sense to me anymore. I hated war. I hated the Germans for what they were doing to me and to all of us.

10- Still Alive

In the weeks that followed, I couldn't eat or concentrate. This was my second experience with unconsolable grief. A simmering anger was gnawing at my insides. I hated that German who had murdered my Nicole. I hated that German officer who had kidnapped my Wistiti. I felt frustrated, helpless, and immobilized by this fire raging inside my body. I couldn't get Nicole and Wistiti out of my mind. Mother walked around the house looking sad. I wondered if she felt my pain.

I continued to have nightmares. *Nicole is screaming for me in a dark forest. I am desperately searching for her in long tunnels. I hear her voice echoing in my ears. Then, my legs feel like lead, unable to move. I scream, "Nicole, Nicole, I'm here."*

Another nightmare. *I am in a huge dark room, and I hear Wistiti shrieking, while a strange creature moves about and brandishes spears and knives. The monster is coming at me while I stand there, frozen in fear, unable to move, feeling that death is imminent. The knives and swords are being thrust toward me and Wistiti. I'm screaming "Wistiti, Wistiti."* I wake up, drenched with sweat, my heart pounding like a jack hammer.

Father, resuming his fatherly role, was supportive but firm. "This is war, George. These are tough times for all of us. We have to rise above all of this and we have to survive, no matter what."

I was grateful that he was safe and that he had survived and that he was back with us and that I should be satisfied that war, so far, had spared my mother and father.

Even though Mother and I were still reeling from the grief over Nicole and Wistiti, we asked Father to tell us the story of his escape from the German POW camp.

One evening, we sat around the table, sipping coffee and lemonades and Father began his story. "Shortly after being drafted, I was sent to the front lines in an infantry division. They were short of supplies. The officers were poorly informed," he explained, "and they didn't even know where the enemy was. No one knew what was going on. There was chaos in the barracks. Everyone was complaining about the lack of supplies, food, medicines and blankets. Even ammunitions were lacking."

"Well, how did you manage?" asked Mother.

"We didn't. We had little communication with the higher commands. Morale was low," he said, "Grenades and artillery shells were exploding all around us and we didn't know what to do with the wounded without medics around. We got those poor devils drunk with wine and cognac, and while they were screaming in pain from their bloody wounds, we cut off their arms and legs that were dangling in shreds from their bodies."

He paused for a minute and said, "I hope I'm not shocking you."

"Oh, no! We want to hear all about it, Papa."

"Suddenly, the Germans fired their artillery and sent their bombers and their stukas. We fired back and ran for shelter. Our soldiers were collapsing and screaming. We fought as hard as we could."

I could feel Father's rage rising in his tone of voice. He went on. "I don't know what the hell was going on. Our commanding officer, who looked like a kid, didn't either. Our communication with higher commands was cut. Then, all of a sudden, orders came to surrender!"

Mother, Grandfather and I were frozen. Father checked our expressions and, seeing Mother nodding at him, went on. "White flags came up. We put our hands over our head. Germans appeared everywhere. Tanks rolled in from all directions. I didn't know how we were going to get out of this bloody mess!"

Father paused. He looked tired and worn out. But we encouraged him to tell all.

"We were sent to the stalags (POW camps). We were being ordered to march with hands on our heads and we marched for hours and hours. They told us that we were prisoners-of-war, and that we were going to detention camps. We were not allowed to speak to one another. Those who disobeyed got kicked in the teeth. They took us to our bunkers and gave us new clothes, rations and water."

"Did they give you enough food?" Mother asked.

"From the start, I began to think about my escape. I knew that there was a chance to do it early before things got too well-organized.

"I was assigned to the kitchen, and luckily they gave the task of carrying food in and out of the compound. I thought this was a real opportunity for a break!

"I made friends with one of the guards, and one day while he was busy, laughing at his own jokes with the other guard at the gate and having a cigarette, I took my chances and sneaked out.

"Before long, it was dark in the forest, and I hid in the thick brush for the night. I figured it would be a while before they would send out a search party with the dogs.

"The next day I ran and walked and ran some more. I never stopped walking until I was halfway across France. I found some good people in a village who gave me food and clothes. They even gave me a bicycle. Then I pedaled my way half way across France until I found you. I am so happy to be home again and to see all of you safe and sound."

He had tears in his eyes and looked like he was choking up and couldn't go on.

He got up and hugged all of us in his long and powerful arms. I would never forget this moment, and I too thanked Providence once more for helping us beat the odds.

* * *

One the night of December 7, 1940, one year before Pearl Harbor, the BBC sent the following message every half hour. "The trumpets are blaring loud and clear."

Although the message sounded ominous, no one could guess what the message really meant unless one had a special code. The answer for the public came the next day.

High flying British planes dropped tracts all over the city, mostly in the harbor area. They announced an imminent bombardment of the entire harbor and implored the civilian population to vacate the area as quickly as possible.

I heard Mother and Father arguing over whether we should move away or not. Mother said, "I think this is a serious warning. Did you read the tracts they dropped this morning? They said that everyone should move away from the harbor to the city center." My father responded, "Nonsense. We have a good and solid cellar that we can rely on if things get tough. Those Brits do precision bombing, not like the Germans who drop bombs mostly to scare people."

Mother lost the argument, and we stayed in the house.

The next night, sirens started wailing and warned us against the British air raid, as announced in the tracts that we had read two days before.

The dark night lit up with searchlights sweeping the sky, as if the city was preparing for an eerie light show.

In total defiance, I stepped out in the street to watch this carnival atmosphere, feeling fearless and excited at the prospect of witnessing a possible dogfight in the sky above me.

As I was pacing back and forth in front of the bar restaurant, I heard mother's shrilling voice calling: "George, George, get in here quick. We're all going to the cellar."

She had barely finished her call when the first bombs started falling. I felt the blast and was lifted off the ground several feet before I was dropped like a sac of potatoes across the street. I was convinced that Mother was right and, crouching while holding my arms over my head to shield against raining stones, I ran into the house and down to the cellar.

Mother had laid down some blankets on the cold cellar floor. We huddled, surrounded by hundreds of the best wine bottles in France.

Father joked, saying "If we get hit, we'll die happy in the best wine bath money can buy!" I don't think that Mother appreciated his macabre humor. I think that she looked angry at him for his having resisted the idea of moving away.

Above our heads, we could hear the whistling of diving bombers followed by huge explosions nearby.

"Merde!"(shit) This one was real close!" Mother yelled.

The blasting of bombs continued without interruption for what seemed to be several hours. The whole house was trembling, and I wondered how much more the walls could take without cracking and collapsing.

We were trapped in this cave as the bombs were getting closer and closer and we could feel the ground shaking under our feet like an earthquake that would not stop.

Bottles began to break, and the wine started gushing on the floor, forming blood-colored rivulets, much to our consternation. All this expensive wine gone to waste!

My father, trying to keep us calm, said, "Those damn British. They don't know how much we care about wine. What are they doing, wasting all that good stuff."

But how ridiculous it was to worry about expensive wines. What about the price of lives? Did he have a warped sense of humor?

The night seemed endless. My ears were hurting from the noise and my eardrums felt as if they were about to burst under the pressure from the blasts. We all hugged each other, as a bomb fell a few yards away.

I was truly frightened and wondered if we would live to see the morning. I thought back to the night of May 20th, 1940, when Oma died in the air raid.

Was *this* going to be the night of our death? We'd never see the end of this war! What a shame! Damn! Why did Father stubbornly resist moving away? Why did Mother listen to him? She wanted to move away. Why didn't she listen to her instincts? Was she always going to give into him? Was this the last time? The noise was unbearable. I would never like Bastille Day again, I thought, or any other fireworks celebrations! Although Mother was not religious, she began to pray for mercy and hope for our survival. How strange it is that people become religious when they are about to die, even if they've never prayed before.

I reached the point where I was resigned to die with my family. Should I say good-bye to them? I feared my father wouldn't take me seriously and would turn the whole thing into another joke. How could he be so stupid? Too bad, I'll never have the guts to tell him how stupid he was.

As the raid continued through the night, I felt a total sense of doom and hopelessness. Mother was holding me so tightly that I could hardly breathe.

Then, in the early morning hours when we were reaching a state of total exhaustion, the air suddenly became silent. The planes had disappeared, the anti-aircraft artillery had stopped, and the last bottles of wine had stopped trickling under our feet.

Father, Mother, Grandfather and I ran upstairs to assess the damage. There were cracks in the walls around us. Part of the ceiling was hanging down, revealing a black hole in the attic. Dust was everywhere; a smoky and tart smell pervaded the entire restaurant.

Tables and chairs were scattered as if a huge brawl had taken place. Broken glasses behind the counter where all the aperitif bottles were shattered off the shelves and onto the floor. Nothing left to sell, I thought. The refrigerator door was ripped open and food and milk bottles were splattered all over the kitchen floor.

In back of the house, there was a huge crater, the size of a city skating rink. The front of the house had slid several inches onto the street, which showed cracks large enough to engulf a truck. Debris littered the streets and broken glass was strewn everywhere.

Cars were torn to pieces and lone tires were rolling down towards the pier. Ships in the harbor were on fire and others were engulfed in huge clouds of black smoke. A peanut factory across the harbor was in flames, and the whole neighborhood smelled like a peanut dump.

A few German and Italian soldiers were walking around the harbor, asking people to clear the area. Ambulances would pick up the wounded. Dead soldiers and sailors lay along the pier, still bleeding from their horrific wounds.

Civilians were walking in a daze, searching for loved ones or lost belongings. Although the rubble made walking difficult, people continued to search and dig their way through piles of debris. A few people were crying and moaning, but most remained silent. Others were calling for relatives caught under the rubble.

As Mother, Father and I walked around, we couldn't be sure whether any of the voices coming from behind the rubble were familiar to us.

My arms were bloody red as were my pants, and Mother looked alarmed, asking me if glass fragments had cut me inside. I reminded her that it was wine, that expensive wine had seeped through my pants, not blood.

War was again hitting home. Was there any hope that this carnage would stop? How much more would we have to endure before the end? How many of us would have to die before this grotesque joke on mankind came to an end?

Papa

Bertha, my mother

Aunt Toni

My friend Henri

Cousin Betty

George M. Burnell, M.D.

My Father

Uncle David

Cousin Dolph, U.S. Army

Family reunion, September 1944. Clockwise: Dolph, Ethel, Opa

Figure 1George, 1944

Figure 2George and Betty, 1943

GrandPa, Toni. Eddy, Dolph

Figure 3Granpa, Opa

George and Jacques

11- The Secret Cellar

After the last bombing raid, our restaurant at the harbor was beyond repair. The building was leaning forward and would crumble if anyone dared piss against the wall.

Father and Mother decided to move and buy two restaurants, one for him and one for her, I guess. They named his restaurant "Le Vignoble" (The Vineyard), and hers "Le Raisin Blanc" (The White Grape) both in keeping with the wines of the region.

They chose to locate on "Cours de la Marne", the street facing the Gare St Jean, the main train station in Bordeaux. It was a calculated choice because all the German troops would get off at the station before being stationed in Bordeaux or shipped out.

Many of the German officers who had come to the old harbor restaurant returned with a smile, as if they were coming home to "Muti Bertha" (Mother Bertha) as they called her affectionately.

The daily routine at home seemed to have returned to normal, except that the war continued in full force. Father was happy again, fixing things around both restaurants and singing Mother's favored arias.

German soldiers came in to flirt with our new waitresses (the old ones had opted to stay near the harbor) drink their cognac and smoke their cigars after a sumptuous dinner. In the course of the evening, Mother would entertain the soldiers in her authentic German, translating the menu from French to German to help the waitresses. Father kept a low profile in the kitchen and backyard.

Business grew to a full and successful enterprise. By doing business with Germans, we had no trouble getting eggs, butter, meat, potatoes, cigars and lots of cognac and schnapps, which the soldiers liked after dinner. At the bar, I pretended not to understand German. I could make out most of what they were saying and I held a deaf ear to their request for service. They must have thought that I was a brat and they sympathized with Mother for having to put up with me.

Father preferred to stay away from them and pretended that they were a nuisance just like the rats and mice in the cellar.

I began to sense that something strange was happening around our house because Father mysteriously disappeared in and out of the cellar several times a day and almost every evening.

I thought he was getting cases of wine and beer for the customers, but as he came up empty handed each time, I decided to investigate.

One day I hid in the cellar and waited patiently in total darkness behind a few beer barrels. I saw Father come down, turn on the single light bulb dangling from the ceiling and carefully open a large trunk and put on some earphones. "Allo, allo. Station 76. This is André. Can you hear me? Can you hear me?" Silence. Father's voice resumed, "I hear you. We're expecting the delivery as usual. Over." He put the earphones down and, as he turned around he saw my shadow on the wall. "George, George. What are you doing here? You're not supposed to be here."

"I know, but I couldn't help wonder what this is all about," I blurted out.

"You must promise me that you'll keep this our secret. No one knows except Mother. George, we are in the Resistance. Understand? No one, you hear me, no one must know…"

"Yes, Papa, I swear."

"Every week, we'll be hiding French paratroopers in our cellars. They'll come after midnight, stay just for a day or so and then go on with their mission. Understand."

"Yes, I do."

I felt good at knowing that Father could trust me, that I could take part in the war effort, and that I could help Mother spy in the restaurant. War was dangerous all right, but it had its exciting moments worth living for. The trick was to be able to survive it all.

* * *

As weeks passed, contingents of armed French undercover agents came into our cellar, usually after midnight. I would wait in the dark at the top of the stairs, listen for their footsteps and try to estimate how many men were in the group. Sometimes, there were five, sometimes seven, and once even up to eleven.

No one knew that every night, at about eleven o'clock, Father and I would go down to our cellar and listen to the latest communiqué of the BBC, thus keeping up with the latest news from the Allied Forces.

It was daring I thought as carousing German officers were still eating, drinking and singing in the restaurant, one flight above us. But the loud phonograph with German records would take care of the camouflage. And Mother made sure that they were properly entertained, wined and dined, while cavorting with the waitresses.

Downstairs, sitting next to Father and listening to the short wave radio, I was amused by the cryptic and imaginative messages from the French Resistance. 'The whales are basking in the sun,' or 'The elephants will blow their noses' and so many others.

Father seemed to know the code for these messages, but he wouldn't let me know what they meant.

"It's time for you to go to bed, George"

I knew that it was useless to argue with him and I obliged, knowing that another contingent of French paratroopers was due that night.

*   *   *

One early morning, I awoke suddenly as the telephone rang three times, then stopped. No one answered. Then, several knocks on the back door. Whispers in the dark. Beams of flashlight dancing on the walls leading to the cellar. Footsteps on the creaky parquet floor. The cellar door swinging open. I peered through my door and saw large shadowy figures slip through the back door, one by one.

I knew that Mother would tiptoe down to the kitchen, work there for a half hour and then carry a big basket of food down to the cellar.

Sitting at the top of the staircase, I heard more whispers, static and voices coming from a radio which, I thought, was the BBC. I leaned over the ramp and saw as many as five or six men slipping in and out of the cellar, whispering to each other. They were all dressed in black and wore weapons on their shoulders. Some carried heavy crates probably loaded with ammunitions and explosives.

I wondered if Father wasn't taking too much of a risk by harboring these men. What if someone found out? What would they do to us? Would they shoot us? Send us away? We had had enough trouble so far, so why ask for more?

Yet, another voice deep inside my brain kept saying, "Don't be so selfish. We all have to help in this war. It's our responsibility, our duty, our pride, our self-respect."

I decided to go back to bed, satisfied that I had had my internal debate on the issue. I think my dead brother, David, once more, had expressed himself in his own mysterious way. The matter was settled, and life would simply go on.

12- Yellow Stars

In January 1942, de Gaulle sent a special emissary, the former Chartres prefect Jean Moulin, into France with the mission to organize and consolidate the growing number of underground resistance groups.

In 1941, de Gaulle had concentrated his efforts on organizing the Free French Liberation Forces (F.F.I.) outside of France, and these dedicated groups ultimately fought side-by-side with the allies in every theater of operations. But by 1942 he had come to understand that the key role was played by the resistance movements working inside France itself.

Although Moscow recognized de Gaulle as the only legitimate leader of all forces fighting inside and outside France, his popularity was not universal. In fact, he was disliked by the US government, especially by President Roosevelt and Secretary of State Hull, who both thought that de Gaulle was offensively pompous.

As a neutral power in 1940, the United States had actually recognized the Vichy government as a legitimate power, which would have made the recognition of Fighting France a rather awkward political move.

De Gaulle further irritated the British and the Americans by stating that all Vichy supporters were traitors, and only he could lead France to liberation.

Fortunately for de Gaulle, his position gained more credibility as Jean Moulin was able to consolidate all the various underground factions under one organization named the National Resistance Council (C.N.R.).

This new organization became the unified fighting guerrilla force inside France, now under the command of de Gaulle's Fighting France.

From 1942 on Free French agents were being parachuted all over France, finding shelter and help from local French citizens.

Some of these paratroopers found their way to our cellar where they could rest, regain their strength, get fed and move on with their mission.

* * *

Meanwhile, European countries were crumbling like cookies falling on the ground. By April 1941, Germans had invaded Yugoslavia and Greece.

German troops marched into Belgrade on March 13, and five days later Yugoslavia surrendered.

By May 1st, all of Greece was occupied. Stopping at nothing, the German army was getting ready to take on Russia, and 90% of its army was now locked in combat on a frontier that extended from the Arctic Ocean to the Black sea.

On December 5th, while only 15 miles from the Kremlin, the Germans were driven out of Moscow, the first time that they had had to retreat since the beginning of the war!

Was this going to be a real turning point? A reversal in this wild conquest of the world? No one knew. But the BBC news of the German retreat was something to cheer about for the first time since the beginning of this ordeal.

Two days later, the radio reported bad news. On December 7th the Japanese attacked Pearl Harbor, and the U.S. responded by declaring war on Japan.

Beginning in September the Nazi Full Solution was in full swing: 39,000 Jews had been machine-gunned in the ravine at Babi Yar and by December 8th the mass gassing of Jews had taken place in the woods of Chermno, Poland.

Over the following months, 350,000 Jews from 200 communities were taken into vans whose exhaust leaked into the sealed interiors, thus serving as mobile gas chambers.

Killing, murdering, and slaughtering were taking place at a hideous pace. Rumors circulated, and some informed sources later said that, although U.S. officials had had wind of these mass executions, the government's decision was to keep this as classified information, not to be disclosed to the public.

On December 11 Germany and Italy declared war on the U.S., and the U.S. in turn declared war on them.

December 22, Churchill came to Washington to meet with FDR, and both agreed to pool their resources under a common command and give their first priority to war in Europe.

* * *

In France, the situation for Jews was taking a bad turn. The Vichy government created a commission to review the status of Jewish immigrants who had entered France since 1927.

Only children born of French fathers could engage in the practice of law and medicine. This was only the first step in a series of restrictive edicts.

By October 4, Vichy had issued a new statute. From then on, foreign Jews were to be arrested and detained in French concentration camps and French Jews were barred from top positions in the public service, the officer corps and noncommissioned officers to professions that influenced public opinion, teaching, the press, radio, film and the theater.

George M. Burnell, M.D.

By March 1941, the Vichy government had created a special office called the Commissariat-General for Jewish Affairs, under the direction of Xavier Vallat, a well-known, ruthless anti-semite, who believed that Jews could never be assimilated. Bad news for the Jews was accelerating.

On May 14, Vichy French Police rounded up 3,700 Jews, arrested them and reviewed their civil status. Most of them were sent to French concentration camps at Pithiviers and Beaune-la-Rolande and later deported to Auschwitz.

In the Second Jewish Statute, measures were taken to limit Jews to two percent of the liberal professions. Only three percent of students enrolled in institutions for higher education.

This was also the first time that such a Statute called for a detailed census of Jews in the Unoccupied Zone, a fatal step for those who fell into the trap, because most were deported.

On July 22, a new "aryanization" law empowered the state "to place all Jewish property in the hands of non-Jewish trustees who had the authority to liquidate it if it was deemed unnecessary to the French economy or to sell it to a non-Jewish purchaser."

In August and December, Germans began to round up Jews as hostages who were to be executed in reprisal for communist agitation or for anti-German attacks carried on by the Resistance. Anytime German soldiers were killed at the hands of the Resistance, Jews were executed the next day as reprisals.

* * *

Things were to get worse for the Jews in France. In January 1942 at the so-called Wannsee Conference plans were made for the "Final Solution" for each European country.

For France, the figure was 865,000 Jews to be eliminated. This was to be broken down into 165,000 from the occupied zone and 700,000 from the unoccupied zone.

In July 1942, the Germans with help from the French police launched their first massive roundup of Jews in Paris. Four thousand Jewish children were snatched from their parents and herded into the Velodrome d'Hiver, a sports stadium in Paris. They were left for five days without water, adequate food or sanitation. When church leaders, for the first time, complained to Vichy's government and begged Pierre Laval, the puppet French Premier appointed by the Germans, to intervene, he refused. The children's suffering had no effect on him. "They all must go," he said.

The children were deported from the transit camp at Drancy along with 70,000 other Jewish victims.

The Germans wanted to make believe that these deportations were for labor convoys and set age limits between sixteen and forty years of age. This was later changed to include children from age two on up.

Louis Danquier de Pellepoix was named commissioner-general of Jewish questions.

Laval named Pierre Bousquet the new secretary general in the Ministry of the Interior. It was he who later requested that the pending deportations of Jews from the Occupied Zone be extended to Jews in the Unoccupied Zone.

He ordered that from age of six upwards Jews must wear the Yellow Star in the Occupied Zone, but under pressure from French politicians, he conceded that in the Unoccupied Zone, Jews need only register with the local French Police.

*   *   *

My parents had never been religious, and although Mother acknowledged her Jewish ancestry in private, she never admitted it in public. Being Jewish had never been a matter for discussion in our household, and Father, a free-mason, openly voiced his position as an atheist. Yet, when the edict to register as a Jew came out, the matter came up for discussion, while I eaves-dropped behind the kitchen door.

"Why would you want to register?" said Father in an angry voice.

"You don't know what they would do if they found out," said Mother."

"You are wearing a cross, posing as a German. We're helping with the FFI (French Free Forces), and you're talking about reporting yourself as a Jew? C'mon. Get back to your senses, Bertha."

"I guess you're right. It's even silly for me to bring it up."

The matter was settled. Registering with the French Police would have been putting a nail in our coffin.

Much to my chagrin, my friends Marcus and Joshua along with their family had decided to register despite all the warnings from my family and me. They were law abiding citizens and they didn't want to break the law. They were going to obey the new edict.

Did they realize what a dangerous course of action they were choosing for themselves? They were afraid of being discovered by neighbors, who might denounce them to the authorities and therefore, they said that they had no choice except to register. I never heard from them again.

*   *   *

Each night at eleven o'clock Father and I would go down to the cellar and listen to the next batch of cryptic messages. Father didn't tell me what these bulletins meant, and I had to figure out for myself if any of them represented a new danger for us.

But even if I thought that danger was imminent, would Mother believe me? Father most likely would minimize it, as he always did, and I would lose more credibility.

I thought 'What if the message was to bomb the railroad station across the street? Should we leave the area? Or leave the city for good? That would arouse suspicion, no doubt. Would the German authorities be wondering why we were leaving? Would the neighbors think that something unusual was going on?'

I had the feeling that neighbors were watching us closely. After all, what were all these high ranking officers doing in and out of our restaurants? Did they think we were collaborators and that our day of reckoning would come after the Liberation? Or did they suspect that our restaurants were a cover-up for a secret Resistance operation? Whatever they thought, it meant potential trouble for us. This was very risky business. Trouble could come from the Germans or from the French, and we had no way of knowing who our real enemies were. Perhaps the real danger lay with the British and the Americans who might be ready to bomb again?

13- The Demarcation Line

I knew that something was terribly wrong when a German officer came to our restaurant and handed a summons to Mother that she and Father had to report to the Kommandantur on Monday morning for routine questioning. He would not elaborate, but his tone of voice was brusque and threatening, implying that we were in big trouble. I heard him as I was coming down the stairs from my room. I had hid in the hallway so I could listen to my Father and Mother's reaction.

The minute he left, my Mother told my Father:

"I believe they're on to something about us. I don't think we can take a chance. Someone must have talked. We've got to leave right away!"

My mother's mind was like a radar, constantly turned on. She could detect danger long before anyone else would suspect it, like a dog picking up suspicious scents from an invisible enemy or a killer at large.

My Father, in his usual skeptical way, retorted.

"Don't be silly. I don't think they can touch us. We've got good references and we have friends in high places."

"But you don't understand. I think they know about what's going on in our cellar. I'm afraid one of the waitresses squealed on us, and they know about the paratroopers and our connection with the Resistance," said Mother.

"What makes you think any of them would do such a thing?" replied Father.

"I had an argument with Helen the other day, and she walked out very upset." Mother said.

"What was it about?"

"As you know, George had been dating her daughter, and I wanted to put an end to this. So, I asked her to speak to her daughter and asked her to stay away from our son," Mother said.

"But it's up to George to stay away from her!" Father said.

"Yes, but I think the daughter leads him on."

"Do you think that she would be so stupid to squeal over a thing like that?"

"I can't be sure. But it seems that this trouble is coming a few days after our discussion"

"But a discussion is not grounds for such a threat," Father said.

"I'm afraid I went a little too far in trying to convince her," Mother replied.

"What do you mean 'went a little too far'?"

"I told her that if they didn't stop seeing each other, I would ask her to leave."

"You mean you threatened to fire her?"

"Yes, I'm afraid I did, and now I'm just so afraid, André."

"That was stupid, Bertha. But I am willing to take my chances. I am a good French citizen," he said as he stood up almost at attention, "and we have a good lawyer, and they will not touch me!"

Yes, but we are Jewish too. We didn't register, and that may be the worst thing they'll hold against you, besides being a spy!"

"Well, I'm not Jewish. I'm an atheist and a free-mason," he said as his voice was getting louder, "and I'm also a Frenchman. You can leave with George and Opa if you wish, but I'm staying. I'll manage the restaurant until you come back!"

My mother looked resigned and defeated. Again, she had run out of arguments against Father. I wondered what she would decide for the rest of us.

I felt terrible about the whole thing. Was I responsible for this new calamity? It's true, I had been dating Michele, the lovely daughter of a new waitress named Helen. Actually, I had been more attracted to Helen, who was a gorgeous woman, but given our age differences— about fifteen years—I had settled for her daughter who was pretty and gentle. Michele and I had been dating for several months, and she had taught me how to kiss and how to fondle on the bottom of a rowboat we used to rent at the lake of the Jardin Public. I loved the long walks we took hand-in-hand, along the quais bordering the Garonne river, and the rue St Catherine where we window shopped, and the long kisses we shared on the Pont de Pierre (Stone Bridge), while the wind was messing up our hair.

My first romance was leading to a terrible blunder. Why didn't Mother talk to me about her concern with Michele? Why did she speak to Helen rather than me? Even Father didn't know about the matter. Was Mother at the root of this awful fiasco? Should I have called Michele or Helen to get to the truth? I was afraid this would compound the matter.

I was angry at Mother for interfering in my life but didn't know how to bring some closure that would satisfy Mother, Father and me. Anyhow, I chose not to call Michele or Helen.

Years later I saw clearly how a simple family matter could intertwine with a life-threatening political situation in war time. Poor family communication could lead to disastrous consequences without any of us aware of it.

* * *

That afternoon, Mother turned to Opa and me and said, "Let's go pack our things. I don't think we have much time."

Opa nodded and winked at me, as if saying, 'Doesn't that sound familiar?'

"I know someone who can get us across the Demarcation Line into the Unoccupied Zone where we'll be safe, but first, I'll have to make a few phone calls," Mother said.

"But Mother, how can we leave. We don't have time to pack all our things."

"All you need is just a suitcase that you can carry yourself. A few clothes, your toothbrush, and your pajamas. That's all. Don't give me any argument. I don't have time to discuss it with you," said Mother.

Opa didn't need much convincing. He had been through this routine several times since the beginning of the war, and I think he knew that time was critical when a threat was imminent.

After dark, we said our goodbyes to Father, still adamant in his decision to stay, and we rushed to the Gare St Jean, only a bloc away, and boarded the last train going south to a small village near the Demarcation Line, a couple of hours south of Bordeaux.

We arrived late that night after many interminable stops. At the station, we met two men, dressed like farmers, who drove us in an old truck to a house a few kilometers from the center of the village. After a brief introduction and appropriate passwords, one of the men said, "It's a good thing you called today, because we don't cross the Line every day. Maybe a couple of times a week. We usually change the time and the days, so the krauts won't get on to our routine. It's been getting harder and harder. This week, we decided to…"

My mother interrupted him. "How do we cross? Is there any danger? How much will it cost?"

One of the two men, the taller of the two, who seemed to be the leader, answered in a gruff voice. "We'll cross after their midnight patrol. We hope they don't shoot at us. They sometimes do when they hear something suspicious going on in the underbrush. I guess they do this to scare people. Oh, yeah. Price? I told you, we'll need 5,000 francs for each of you."

Mother didn't argue and handed over the money in cash.

Although we were exhausted, we decided not to sleep for fear of being unprepared in case the men decided to leave earlier.

"You people wait out here in the living room. We'll get our stuff ready and wire our friends across the border to make sure they are ready to make contact with us," the leader of the men said.

My mother and Opa nodded their approval.

At about 1 a.m., the call came and gave the all-clear signal. The two men, armed with rifles, turned to us and said, "It's time to go. Are you sure you can carry your stuff? We'll have to keep our hands free in case there is trouble."

"We'll carry our stuff," said Mother.

We left the house in total darkness. The thick forest ahead was quiet except for crickets stridulating in the field and an owl hooting. We climbed into an old truck, and the men drove us to a designated point five or six kilometers away.

The air was cool and damp. My fingers were numb, and I could feel my heart pounding in my chest. The men gestured to us, pointing to a small path ahead.

Carrying our suitcases, Opa, Mother and I trailed behind the two men who whispered to us to keep very quiet.

"We'll be waiting for a signal," one of the men muttered.

We stood there, feeling totally at the mercy of these two strangers. I began to ruminate. Could we really trust them after they got our money? Would they hand us over to the authorities? Or would they keep their promise and save us?

Within a few minutes, out of the pitch black forest ahead of us, we heard a peculiar whistle which was repeated three times. The men responded to the signal with a hooting sound. One of the men whispered, "We'll be crossing the border now. Just be sure to walk very quietly. No talking please."

My mother clutched my arm so tightly that it almost hurt. Opa stayed behind us as we walked like overloaded donkeys.

Only the sound of crushed dead leaves under our feet was breaking the silence of the night.

In the distance, we heard rifles being fired in the dark. The shots seemed to be getting closer and closer as we made our way through the thick brush. The men walked steadily along the path and didn't need any flashlight. Just the muffled sound of their footsteps was enough to guide us.

We heard shots being fired nearby. The men stopped walking and hushed us.

My brain was whirling with worrisome thoughts. Had we been found out? Was it a trap? A set-up? We had heard rumors that some French folks had made a nice profit by turning refugees over to the Germans? Was that going to be the end of our journey?

Suddenly, the firing stopped. We resumed our walk. This time, hurrying like mice fearful of being caught and slaughtered.

After a few minutes, which seemed endless, we met another two men and a woman, waiting by a lake. One of the men said, "Did you run into any trouble? We heard several shots."

"No, the krauts were trying to scare some birds. They shoot them when they are bored, you know," said one the men.

"Welcome to the free zone," said the woman, while extending her hand to Mother and Opa. "C'mon over to our house, and we'll give you some warm blankets, hot soup and a place to sleep."

We all breathed a sigh of relief, feeling that now we were free and safe at last.

"To-morrow morning, we'll take you to the village station on the other side, and you can catch the train to Toulouse. You're free people, now. Good night and sleep well," said the woman.

14- The Wrong Train

After breakfast, the woman drove us to the small train station on the other side of the border in the non-occupied zone. She wished us good luck and left us in front of the station.

"Your train should be arriving soon. It gets in by eight o'clock," she said, as she waved good bye. She seemed in a hurry to leave, as if she didn't want to be seen with us.

The station was deserted. Not a soul. It was spooky like a ghost town. There were no signs on the two platforms to show us where to wait for the next train. Local folks must have known where trains came from, where they were heading to, and which platforms to go to. We asked ourselves where the station master was. The ticket window was closed. There was no clerk in sight. No repairman walking around. Only a few abandoned trucks in the parking lot. A eerie silence enveloped the entire station. The sun was visible between the clouds, barely warming the cool morning air.

We sat on two little wooden benches next to our suitcases, looking in both directions, watching for a train.

"Where do you want to go?' Opa asked Mother.

"I guess we'll stop in Toulouse and look around."

"Do you know anyone there?" said Opa.

"Well, yes. Don't you remember that David, Ethel and Betty finally left Paris and decided to go to Toulouse? said Mother.

I jumped in the conversation. "Will I start school there again?"

"I don't know. It all depends," said Mother.

"Depends on what?" I said.

"Depends on whether we can find a place to live there," said Mother.

Opa decided to help Mother with these questions. "Don't worry, George. Mother will do what's best for all of us, you know."

I sensed it was best to leave it at that. We all remained quiet. But the silence was most unsettling, as we kept looking into one direction, then the other, like fearful cats sensing danger ahead.

A long hour passed before a train finally arrived. It was a quarter after eight. Was it late? Why did the woman say the train would get in by eight?

We boarded the train with a mixture of excitement and residual fear from the night before. We had no tickets. We would pay our fare directly to the ticket master when he'd come by to check passengers in the compartments.

We heard the train whistle and, breathing a sigh of relief, we sat back in our seats. Finally, we were on our way to Toulouse, free and safe.

The ticket master came along.

"Tickets, please."

"We don't have our tickets. We'd like to buy them now," said Mother.

"Where to?" said the ticket inspector.

"Toulouse, please."

"Well, madam. That's not possible. This train is going the other way. It's going to Bordeaux, and our next stop is at the "Demarcation Line," he said in a terse voice, "and you'll need all your papers in order. You understand?"

My mother became pale, and I thought she was going to pass out. Opa, who didn't understand what the ticket master said, but seeing Mother's face, took her arm and squeezed it, as a signal to keep quiet.

The train inspector didn't charge us for the tickets, accepting that we had made an honest mistake in taking the train in the wrong direction.

Since we were the only ones in the compartment, Mother, Opa and I decided to have a conference.

"What are we going to do?" said Opa.

"Are they going to arrest us at the border?" I asked Mother. She didn't answer directly.

"We could just jump off the train while we are still in the free zone," said Mother.

"But the train is going too fast. We would all get hurt, and then, where would we go for help?" asked Opa, "Well, maybe just the two of you could jump. I am an old man. There isn't much they could do to me. I speak German, and that might help."

"There's no way we'd let you do this. We've got to find a solution," said Mother.

"Maybe we can go back to the farmers in the village, and start all over with them," I said to Mother.

"Wouldn't that be risky for them?" said Mother.

"Can we make up a story to the authorities?" asked Opa.

"Yes, but what?" Mother and I asked at the same time.

Meanwhile, the train was approaching the station at the border. It was too late to consider the jumping off solution.

The ticket inspector had wandered off. Maybe he could have intervened on our behalf, explaining that we had accidentally taken the wrong train and that we were local folks on their way to visit relatives in Toulouse. We searched frantically for him but he was nowhere to be found.

The train pulled into the station.

German soldiers were milling around everywhere, walking back and forth, holding their rifles across their chest in a ready-to-shoot stance.

We heard a loud, harsh voice.

"Aussteigen, aussteigen. Papiere, Papiere. Schnell, schnell!"

Mother regained her senses. Opa was praying quietly. I was wondering how all this would end. Where were we going to sleep tonight? In jail? Back to Bordeaux? Worse yet, would they simply shoot us if they found out we had run away from the Kommandantur in Bordeaux?

As we were being escorted to a separate building next to the main station, getting ready to present our identification papers, we heard a voice coming from the other side of the platform.

"Frau Meyer, Frau Meyer, was machen Sie denn hier?" (Mrs. Meyer, what are you doing here?)

A German officer, in full dress uniform, smiling broadly, was approaching us, obviously eager to speak to Mother. She recognized him as one of her most faithful customers at the restaurant.

"Oh, mein guter Oberleutnant, Ich bin so gluckich Sie hier zu sehen sie." (My dear colonel, I am so fortunate to see you.)

"Kann ich Ihnen behilflich sein?" (Can I be of any help to you?)

Then, she explained in her authentic German.

"You see, my father, my son and I are on our way to see an old aunt, who is very ill and lives in Toulouse. But we took the wrong train, and now we need to change trains to get back in the right direction. We'll only be gone for a week."

The German colonel shouted to the examining officer, "Lasst diese Leute zufrieden. Ich kenne sie. Sie brauchen nicht geprueft werden."(Leave this party alone. I know them. No need to check them), as he signaled us to cross the tracks to the other side.

He then turned to Mother and in half French, half German, he said, "Your train should be here any minute. Be sure to get back to Bordeaux soon because I like your cooking. You make the best Wienershnitzel a la Holstein. Auf Wiedersehen, Frau Meyer!" And he waved us on.

15- Toulouse

Toulouse is a charming city on a wide bend of the river Garonne, midway between the Atlantic and the Mediterranean, and it is the economic and intellectual center of the region. It's also known as the "pink city" because of the color of its brick houses.

We arrived in Toulouse in the late afternoon and met with Uncle Dave and Aunt Ethel, who had fled there from Paris a few months before. They were renting a two bedroom apartment on a month-to-month basis, undecided as to where they would eventually settle.

"This is a small place, but you can take the small guest room, and George, you can sleep in the living room," said Ethel as we all sat around the coffee table in the living room.

Mother was fidgety, and immediately asked, "Ethel, I've got to call Bordeaux. I haven't heard from André yet."

"Please, call him, and let us know what's going on," said Ethel.

Mother called the restaurant, but there was no answer. She tried a few hours later, but no answer from Father or anyone else for that matter.

155

Mother and I began to speculate. Did he come back after his appointment at the Kommandantur? Did they keep him? It would not be safe to call on the neighbors because we didn't trust them to tell us the truth.

Mother called our lawyer, Mr. Broca, whose office was in downtown Bordeaux. He had been a faithful friend over the years, and although it was a risk, Mother said that she hoped that his leanings were with the Free French.

Mr. Broca, an attorney in his prime, was a tall and husky man with thick glasses, a deep cavernous voice, and a gentle smile. He boasted about having many connections among the Bordeaux high officials and political figures of the time. More importantly, he got along well with us, especially with my father, who trusted and relied on him.

I couldn't wait to hear news about Papa. So, Mother let me listen on the other line, to her conversation with Mr. Broca.

"Allo, Mr. Broca. This is Mrs. Meyer."

"Bonjour madame. What can I do for you?"

"I am in Toulouse now with my son and father. André has been summoned to the Kommandantur on Monday morning, and I haven't heard from him since we left. I tried to call our restaurant, but there was no answer. Is there anything you can do to look into this matter?"

"Well, yes, I know some people at City Hall and at the Prefecture. I'll give them a call right away. Do you want me to call you back?"

"No, I can't give you my phone number or address. You understand that we are running away and..."

"Yes, I understand. Call me back in a day or so. I'll see what I can find out."

Mother didn't look appeased by Mr. Broca's answers. Deep inside, my inner voice was also telling me that trouble was brewing again. Was Papa in serious danger? If so, why did he not come with us? Why wasn't Mother able to convince him to join us? All these questions were reverberating in my brain, like flies buzzing around my head. If Mother had talked to me about Michele, maybe none of this would be happening.

Mother could see my distress, but was so upset herself that she found no immediate way to reassure me.

We were exhausted and we turned in early that night.

* * *

Two days later, Mother called Mr. Broca again. She let me listen on the extension line.

"Allo, Mr. Broca. What have you found out?" Mother said.

"Well, André is being held under suspicion of subversive activity. Does André have Jewish blood in his family?" asked Broca.

"I believe his mother was Jewish, but his father was Catholic, or vice-versa. Frankly, I don't remember who was what. It wasn't important to him or to me. He was really an atheist, you know, and he was a freemason. That's all I know," Mother replied.

"I'm afraid that won't help. But I'll do everything I can to intervene, you understand. But you know how strict the Gestapo is, and the French Police says their hands are tied..." Broca said.

"Well, try again Mr. Broca. You're a good man, and maybe they'll listen to you. I'll call you in a few days."

After she hung up, Mother and I agreed that it didn't sound good. She admitted that she was worried for his life.

"I don't like the way Mr. Broca was talking. He sounded pessimistic.

I don't know if I could trust him," Mother said.

That night, the whole family held a conference to review their options and their plans. My uncle and aunt said they were going on to Grenoble, a city in the Alps, and begged Mother and Grandfather to come along.

"You can come with us and if you don't like Grenoble you can move on to Lyon," said David in his typical supportive voice.

"We don't want to burden you," said Mother.

"Nonsense. You're part of this family. You can do as you wish, but I'll be very sorry if you don't come with us now," said David.

David and Ethel said how fortunate we were to be in non-occupied France, the free France so to speak, but expressed doubt that France would remain in this divided status. "The Germans have been known to renege on their promises," said David.

Betty, my cute little cousin, was pleased to see me again. Why did we have to split up again? Can't grown-ups behave like grown-ups? I thought.

Other thoughts were swirling in my head. 'Will my father die? Or is he dead already? Will he escape once more as he did when he was a POW in Germany? I stayed awake all night, trying to find an answer to these impossible questions.

* * *

Before we took the train to Grenoble, Mother called Mr. Broca once more and put me on the extension line. "Allo, Mr. Broca. I hope you have some news for us."

"Yes, I'm afraid I do. André is still incarcerated. They won't allow me or any other lawyer to visit him for that matter. They said they found ammunitions in your cellar and clothes for French paratroopers. Also, they discovered a short wave radio," Broca said.

"Can you do anything to deny those charges?" Mother said.

"I doubt it, as he has already been tried and sentenced. He is scheduled to leave for Drancy for further action..." Broca said.

"But isn't Drancy the place where they send Jews and Communists?" Mother asked.

"I don't really know for sure. But at any rate, I'll be frank with you. It doesn't sound good. The German police have closed your two restaurants and confiscated everything in them. So, I don't advise you to return at this time," Broca continued.

Mother was holding back her tears and looked as if she was choking. After a long pause she managed to get the last few words out.

"Thank you, Mr. Broca. You've been so good to help us. I'll never forget. Thank you again. Perhaps, some day we'll meet again," Mother said, barely able to speak out.

"I wish you the best. Good luck. Take care of yourselves." Broca said with a sad voice and hung up.

* * *

The next day, Mother took me aside and said, "I have something very important to tell you. It's a secret I have kept from you for a long time."

She immediately got my attention. I had no clue what she had possibly kept from me. And what could be so important as to bring it up at this time, when so many things were going on in our lives?"

"What is it, Mother?"

"Well, I've never told you that before. But Papa isn't your real father."

"What d'you mean?" I said, as if I hadn't heard what she said.

"I mean that he is not your real father. I was married to your real father, Marcel, a long time ago. We got divorced, and I married André, who later raised you like his own son. He loved you just the same as a father would. But I thought you ought to know now that you'll be taking official exams in school."

"What should this have anything to do with?" I replied, still not believing what she said.

"Well, you see, your real name isn't Meyer. You should assume your legal name when you take your state exams or your diplomas will not be valid," Mother said.

"What's my legal name, then?

"It's Bercovici. It's a Rumanian name."

I was shocked but tried not to show it.

Was this her way of helping me cope with a possible long separation from Papa? Did she think that we were never going to see Papa again? Was she really concerned about the name change? It was as if more flies were buzzing over my head.

I didn't know what to think or what to ask? I felt confused and resentful, trying to decide on the significance of this revelation. I retreated into my own little world, hoping to find some hidden meaning in all this confusion. Was this really true what Mother said about my diplomas being invalid under a different name? Why did Papa not adopt me? Why did they let me carry his name all these years? Although I was troubled by all these questions, I chose not to dwell on them and confront Mother, thinking that she was still too upset about Papa's news.

Later, I asked Mother: "How long are we going to stay in Toulouse?"

"Oh! I didn't tell you? We're just passing through. We're going on to Lyon or Grenoble. We'll stay with Aunt Ethel and Uncle David only for a few days."

16- Lyon and Grenoble

Mother said she was unsure whether to settle in Lyon or in Grenoble. But finally, after accepting Uncle David's invitation to accompany them, we went on to Grenoble.

I was rejoicing at the thought of being reunited with Betty, my lovely cousin who now looked like Ingrid Bergman, and whom I had missed so much. The prospect of sharing a common apartment with her and her parents really appealed to me.

Grenoble is a charming city with majestic mountains all around. The whole city takes on sharp and crisp colors in the winter and pastel shades in the summer. Walking on the scenic avenues, one can inhale clean, fresh air that reaches deep into the lungs and chat everywhere with friendly people, accustomed to hosting travelers and tourists.

We had arrived in Grenoble on a bright summer afternoon. I liked it as soon as we got there. The scenery was so picturesque that I felt more alive there than anywhere I had lived before. I shared my enthusiasm with Mother and said, "I hope we stay here for a change."

Mother didn't look as though she was listening. To me, she seemed so far away.

"I mean, I'm tired of moving all the time. Why can't we settle down?" I said.

She looked at me with a sad smile and said, "I wish we could, but I don't know if we can make it here."

We spent a couple of months in Grenoble, living with my uncle, aunt and Cousin Betty. It was wonderful. No police at our heels; lots of hiking trails to go on with Betty and Uncle David; breath-taking scenery wherever we looked; a sense of peace and serenity and no evidence of war.

Despite this idyllic setting, Mother became restless again.

I don't remember the reasons why Mother said she wanted to move on to Lyon. Was it truly for business reasons? Was it because of a fight with her sister? Or was it because of the old rivalry between them in playing up to my uncle's good looks?

I didn't want to know. I was sick and tired of having to move again, change school, change friends, and now even change my name!

My main regret about moving was that I wouldn't see Cousin Betty any more. I knew that I'd miss her terribly.

We left at the end of summer so that I could enroll at the lycee (high school) in Lyon and start classes in September.

* * *

Lyon was a much larger city than Grenoble. It was surrounded by the two rivers, Rhone and Saone, that squeezed a strip of land known as the Presqu'ile, which means "almost an island."

These two rivers have totally different personalities. Whereas the Saone is calm, serene and easy-going, the Rhone is spirited, exciting, raging at times, and always crashing down to the South.

Overlooking the entire city are two prominent hills, Fourviere "the begging hill", and La Croix Rousse, "the working hill". On the left bank of the Rhone are the industrial suburbs where two thirds of the people live.

To the north is the famous "Park de la Tete d'Or" with its romantic lakes, shady paths, rolling meadows, and cute hideaways, where I had my most passionate teenage romances.

To the west of the Saone is the "Vieux Lyon" (the old town) with its magnificently preserved Renaissance buildings, and to the east of the Rhone is modern Lyon, where tourism stops and serious business begins.

We found an apartment in the old town, a side street off the rue Merciere, well-known for its tourist shops, and lived there until Mother bought another restaurant on the Avenue Vitton, a busy street lined with tall plane trees in the business section, near the train station "Brotteaux."

We moved into the living quarters on the second floor just above the restaurant. This arrangement was most convenient for Mother, who was a late riser and did not like commuting. As in Bordeaux, I was happy to have a large room all to myself.

The restaurant was a pleasant, cheerful place. Mother and I had debated on what to name the restaurant, and finally we had settled on the name "Le Colibri" which in French, means "The Hummingbird."

In the main dining room, there were large mirrors on the wall and between the mirrors pictures of old movie stars just above the red leather booths. A long bar counter with bar stools on the left side would provide a place to have an aperitif, while waiting for a table. Le Colibri had the atmosphere of the roaring twenties, cheerful and full of life, especially after customers crowded the bar and popular tunes of the twenties and thirties filled the air.

I enrolled at the lycee Ampere, one of the most prestigious schools in Lyon with a rigorous program that demanded high performance from its students and a perfect attendance record. This was fine with me. I always liked school, studying and learning. My grades had always been good, and I passed the entrance exam without difficulty. But, like wearing an uncomfortable new suit that was too tight and ill-fitting, I felt uneasy about my new name, which sounded so strange to me. I couldn't get used to the idea of a new name. I was no longer George Meyer, but George Bercovici. I not only didn't know how to pronounce it, I didn't even know how to spell it.

"Must I really have to keep this name?" I asked Mother.

"Well, if you want your diplomas to be valid, you'll have to keep this name. Later on, when you become an adult, you could change it to whatever you like."

"What? Change it again, when I become an adult?" I said, feeling irked.

I had to admit that Mother was right and that it sounded like a logical explanation. I yielded to common sense and thought, "some day when I have a choice, I'll choose a name I can spell and pronounce "(Little did I know that ten years later I would change it again.)"

I was still brooding over the revelation that André was not my "real father." I couldn't understand why Mother had waited so long to tell me. Did she think that knowing the truth would have jeopardized my relationship with "Papa"? Did she think that it would have helped me cope with his disappearance? Maybe his death? What difference did it really make that he was not my biological father? He had raised me and treated me like his own son. Isn't that what really mattered? Fathers who spend their life away from their children aren't true fathers. Or so I thought.

My so-called "real father" had not been around all these years. I had never gotten to know him, so I saw no point of making this a big issue. I would probably never get to meet him anyway.

I couldn't help wondering what he was like. What did he look like? What did he do in life? Where did he live? Did he remarry? Did he go to war like Papa did? Why did he stay away all these years?

A spate of questions kept flooding my brain as if it had been overtaken by a tidal wave. Questions about my unknown father, questions about my newly-appointed step-father, questions about my Mother's role in their marriage, questions about what had gone wrong in their marriage? And questions about my part in all this complicated history?

Despite these cerebral storms, life in Lyon began as a normal and comfortable routine.

After school, I would take over the bar while Mother tended to the restaurant. Francoise was the pretty waitress with a cute white apron, who helped in both the restaurant and the bar. She was the main attraction for a faithful group of young customers who came to flirt with her and who made me jealous. Francoise had gorgeous blue eyes, silky shoulder-length blond hair, and slender legs which I couldn't ignore every time she bent over to wipe the floors or pick up after the customers. I developed a crush on her. Fearing rejection or complication, I decided not to reveal my yearning for her. I was satisfied with the wild dreams she triggered over the next few months, giving me ample sexual release.

But at the bar I had my own group of fans. A few customers, intellectual types, preferred to engage in a scholarly conversation with me. The range of topics was rather wide: scientific discoveries, foreign policy, national politics, sports, history. I had an opinion on everything.

We stayed away from controversial and dangerous topics: religion, the war, Germans, Jews, and the Resistance.

I would challenge their opinions, which often brought a laugh from the audience, amazed at my fund of knowledge. To Mother they would say, "Your son is not only a handsome guy, he is also a scholar." Mother would smile and reply, "Yes, I know. He is going to be a good doctor some day."

17- A New Father

I had almost forgotten the revelation about my real father when one day, Mother, who had just returned from the market, announced cheerfully, "Guess who I met today in the street?"

I shook my head and said, "I don't have the slightest idea. Please tell me. Don't leave me in suspense like this."

"Well, I met your father, I mean your real father!"

"You mean you met him in the street? Just like that?"

"Yes. It was pure coincidence. I was walking with my grocery bag, and there he was, across the street. I recognized him. I called him 'Marcel, Marcel, it's me Bertha!'"

"No kid'n! I don't believe you," I said, in total disbelief.

"Yes, I tell you. We went for a cup of coffee. He was so nice! And he wants to meet you as soon as possible."

"Well, Mother, I don't think I'm ready for this!"

"I tell you. It's all arranged. We're meeting him tomorrow at noon at a local bistro."

I was dumbfounded. I didn't really know what to think of this whole experience. Meeting my father after 13 years! I couldn't imagine this? It sounded stranger than fiction, the kind of stuff you see in the movies, but not in real life! Was it truly coincidence as mother said, or had she known all along that father was living in Lyon? But then, why would she lie?

All the questions I had asked myself a month ago came back, flooding my brain as if a gigantic cloudburst had exploded inside my head.

Where had he been all these years? What was he doing here in Lyon? Why did Mother and he get divorced? And if they were divorced, why were they so friendly?

My curiosity grew like an intolerable itch. I decided that I should meet him. I had nothing to lose.

* * *

It was on a sunny afternoon with a light breeze and a few clouds floating in the sky. We were late. Maybe five or ten minutes. We were hurrying to the rendez-vous with my so-called real father.

As we approached the busy cafe where he was to meet us, my heart started pounding. Mother and I crossed the street to reach the sidewalk cafe where several couples sat in large rattan chairs aligned in front of small tables.

At one of the tables sat a man in a trench coat. He was wearing a gray felt hat with a brim that covered his forehead. He was smoking a cigarette and reading a newspaper. Steam was coming out of a cup of coffee in front of him.

I thought he looked like a secret agent—some sort of spy. He reminded me of Humprey Bogart or Richard Widmark I had seen in American movies. I thought that he might be an agent working for the Free French Forces. Or perhaps a spy working for the Americans?

Mother nudged me gently towards him and said to him, "Max, this is George, your son."

"I am so pleased to see you, George. It's a great pleasure for me. You're so big and strong. Your mother told me a lot about you. She said that you're good in sports, that you study hard and that you love the movies. Is that true?"

"Yes, it is," I answered sheepishly.

"I know this must be a hard time for you to get settled in a new city, with a new school, new friends, new home."

"Yes, kind of..." I said, thinking to myself that he omitted to mention the darn new name—which happened to be his name.

He looked as though he was straining to make conversation. Mother broke the ice. "We are new in this town but we found a nice place to live near the Saone river, and George has already enrolled at the lycee Ampere, one of the best schools in Lyon."

"Well, I am impressed," said the man who now was posing as my father.

Feeling awkward and uneasy, I started to fidget. My new father saw my discomfort and said, "There's a new movie with Fernandel playing in the theater across the street. Would you like to see it?"

"Yes, I would," I said.

"Well, here is 100 francs. Keep the change!"

I took the money, thanked him and asked Mother if I could go. She approved and I left, relieved that the rendez-vous was over.

* * *

In the months following our awkward introduction, my real father and I became good friends. On occasions, I'd come to visit him in his apartment and spend a night or two on the week-end.

He had an obsession with apples, and truly believed that an "apple a day keeps the doctor away." He would buy cartons of green apples, line them up on the mantelpiece, let them age and then offer them to all the friends who came to visit.

He introduced me to his friends at the synagogue. Although he was not deeply religious, he would go to the services to make contacts and socialize with the local community.

Socializing was an important part of my father's life, and he would often say to me that "valued friends are more important than money in the bank." Lots of people owed him money including many of them who had lost their bad hands at poker. He was good at cards and had played for money over many years. Mother felt that deep down he was a true gambler although he said that he had given up the "habit" a long time ago.

I admired his amazing popularity and his ease in meeting new people. Yet it was precisely this aspect of his personality that had driven Mother away from him. Mother used to say, "Your father has a heart of gold, and he'd give the shirt off his back to anyone in need, but his family would always come second."

Even though the bad memories had dissolved and the old grievances had vanished, the romance between them had faded. The few good trace memories that lingered on were enough to rekindle a platonic relationship and erase whatever grudges or resentment might have sprung up years ago.

*   *   *

I was curious to know how my father and mother had met. Mother had told me her version, but I was interested in hearing his side also.

One day, he told me why he had immigrated to France and how he had met Mother.

We sat down in the living room, and he began his story. "I was born in Romania in a town called Iasi where I lived with my father and mother. Life was harsh because Jews were constantly persecuted. They had no rights. They couldn't travel freely or start a business or hold jobs in government. After I finished school, my parents urged me to leave the country and go to France where there was freedom and opportunities for a good life."

He paused and looked over his half moon glasses to see if I was still interested. Satisfied that he had my full attention, he went on.

"When I reached my 21st birthday, they gave me some money, bought me a new suit, a train ticket to France, and wished me good luck. I didn't know then that I would never see them again."

"Were you scared?" I said.

"Yes, I was. I had never left home before. I had never been on my own. I didn't speak French, but I knew my parents were right to send me away."

"So where did you go?"

"I took the train to Paris where my parents had a friend who had been living there."

"Is that where you met Mom?" I interjected.

"Yeah. She'd just arrived from Vienna. We found we had a lot in common. She and I spoke Yiddish—you can always trust anyone who speaks Yiddish, you know—and we hit it off right away. She was all alone, without money, without friends, no contacts."

"So, what happened?" I asked.

"We fell in love. We started working together. I got a job selling textiles, and we lived very nicely."

"Well, why did you get divorced?"

"It wasn't my idea. She started getting big ideas. She wanted to travel, get a house, start a business. She had ideas of grandeur. And then, you and your twin brother were born," he said, letting out a big sigh, "and then your twin brother died eighteen months later. The doctor said it was meningitis."

"It must have been awful for both of you," I said.

"Yeah. She couldn't be consoled. I felt she was blaming me for not having provided all the things she wanted."

He had made no mention of the gambling habit, of their differences in life goals, of his lack of ambition: all of which Mother had complained.

He paused and went on. "Then, one day, she ran away and took you with her. She left no address. I searched everywhere for months and years but couldn't find her. She disappeared until we met again!"

I was totally mesmerized by the whole story and by his frankness. I felt that I understood him for the first time and that I was getting close to him.

18- The Milice

Lyon turned out to be a friendly city until the Germans decided to occupy the rest of France, and the French Milice began their campaign of plundering and killing Jews. The Milice, a detachment of the French Police, specialized in rounding up Jews, Communists and Resistance fighters who were designated as potential hostages to be executed for reprisals.

I felt strange to see German troops marching down the street, singing their tunes of "Lily Marlene" or "Deutchland Uber Alles." (Germany Will Prevail).

Life was getting complicated again. We had been told to watch out for certain unmarked cars in the street, carrying Milice officers in plain clothes, who were patrolling neighborhoods and picking up people at random or anyone who looked suspicious to them.

One day I returned from school and decided to stop by my father's apartment to pick up some books and various writings I had left there the week before. As a way of dealing with my pent-up rage against the Germans and the French Milice, I had found a good release by writing anti-war and anti-Nazi essays and poetry which I didn't share with anyone, not even with Mother and Father.

As I was climbing the stairs up to the apartment, the landlady, whom my father knew intimately and whom I had gotten to know well, stopped me in the spiral staircase, and said, "George, you better leave right away. The Milice is up there, and they're searching the whole apartment. I called your father to tell him not to come. I think they arrested your grandfather who happened to be visiting."

I turned around and made a dash for the street, worrying that they might find the whole stack of anti-Hitler and anti-Nazi poems and all the essays I had written over the last few months.

I rushed home, worried about what Mother would think about the whole incident, especially about Opa's arrest. I didn't know whether I should keep quiet or whether I should tell her what had happened.

But as I came through the door, I decided to tell her everything I heard from the landlady. Mother became pale and frightened. Imagining the worst for Opa, she looked as if she was going to faint. Then, she regained her composure and said, "We must be extremely careful. Let's hope they will not trace the investigation to our place."

A climate of fear and dread had fallen all over Lyon. It was no longer the friendly city we had known, when we had first arrived. One could no longer trust the neighbor, the baker, the butcher, the grocer, the postman or the delivery boys. Anyone could report a person to the authorities, if they felt any resentment towards that person. It was just like Bordeaux all over again. Three Germans had been ambushed and killed that week.

Hostages were taken randomly in the streets every time German soldiers were wounded or killed by the French Resistance. Assassinations of German or French officials were not uncommon but were immediately followed by reprisals. People whose "identity papers were not in order" were summarily arrested, made hostage, and executed by the Germans. The ratio was usually 3 to 5 hostages for each German killed. Fifteen persons had to be arrested in reprisal.

Fear and panic spread in the city until all the scheduled reprisals were completed. The bodies of the hostages who were shot were laid down on the curbs in a gruesome display for everyone to see, as a reminder that another anti-German transgression could result in anyone's getting picked up, arrested and shot.

That afternoon, Mother and I decided to wait for any new development. We packed a small suitcase in the event that we would have to leave town in a hurry. Mother asked Francoise, our waitress, to answer the phone and take all messages.

We knew from past experience that any call from the authorities would mean that we would have less than an hour to leave the city.

*   *   *

The next day I went to school as usual. During my second class, a course in Latin, a man dressed in a business suit knocked on the classroom door. When the teacher opened the door and inquired, I saw the man lean over and whisper a few words in the teacher's ear. Then the teacher turned to the class, calling my name and said, "George, you are to report to the Principal's office immediately."

A wave of whispers swept across the whole class. I knew that this inquiry was ominous and was probably related to the events at my father's apartment.

I left the class, bolted to the nearest school exit and ran for a streetcar but failed to jump on it.

The man who had come to the classroom door and several other men in plainclothes started to run after me. I sensed that my life would depend on my running ability and skills. I felt that if they caught up with me, that would be the end.

I ran faster and decided to take side streets, and then back to main streets where people were strolling and streetcars were stopping.

I spotted a fast streetcar that was passing nearby. I decided to make a run for it.

The men were still running and seemed to be gaining on me. I neared the streetcar and in an ultimate supreme effort bounded in the air and landed on the last wagon's sideboard.

A man on the platform saw me and said, "Hey, you kid, you're going to kill yourself, doing this sort of thing!"

"No, mister, I'm going to live because I *did* this sort of thing!"

I no longer could see the men in plainclothes behind me. It would be too dangerous to go home and I got off near the Parc de la Tete d'Or, the largest park in Lyon that I knew well and where I could hide safely.

For hours I walked through the park, always looking back to check for any possible pursuers. What would be the best strategy at this point? If Mother had been arrested, what could I do for her?

The Milice would continue their search and I had to find a hiding place for the night.

*   *   *

I remembered what Henri, my best friend, had said to me months ago. "If you ever get into a jam and need a place to stay, just come and stay with us."

He and his parents lived on the outskirts of the city, just a perfect place to hide.

I jumped on the streetcar to Villeurbanne, a suburb of Lyon, and arrived there just in time for dinner. Henri's parents were extremely fond of me and had invited me on many occasions.

As I came through the door, unannounced, they seemed surprised, but, seeing the frightened look on my face, Mrs. Waisblatt asked:

"Why, George, what's happening? What brings you now? We weren't expecting you. Henri didn't say anything about your coming."

"I don't think he even knows that I'm here," I said.

"Well then, dear, tell us…"

"The Milice raided my father's apartment, and I think they are at our house too. They came for me at school today. But I got away."

"Oh! My God. That's terrible. You're welcome to stay with us as long as you wish. We'll take care of you until we know more about your mother, father and grandfather."

Henri arrived from school, and had heard of my escape. The word had gotten out in school that a student who was in big trouble had escaped before the police could catch him at the Principal's office.

I felt safe but intensely worried about Mother, Opa, and my new father.

We all sat down to dinner. Henri was delighted that we were going to have some time together to play more chess and discuss our latest female conquests.

* * *

I was worried sick over Mother and Opa. Henri's mother offered to call the restaurant, and she let me listen on the other line.

"Is Mrs. Meyer there, Francoise? It's Mrs. Waisblatt, a friend of the family."

"No, Mrs. Waisblatt. She's not here. She was arrested this afternoon by the French Police," Francoise said, choking up on her tears.

Before the call could be traced, Mrs. Waisblatt hung up.

I suspected that the Milice had traced my writings to our address. Or perhaps it had been another instance of the work of some collaborators, dirty rats as I called them, who had turned us in for listening to the BBC maybe, or had accused us of being Jewish.

I was overcome with fear, rage and frustration. I couldn't sleep, and my appetite was gone.

"You must eat and get strong," said Henri's mother. "You'll need to be strong to help your mother and grandfather."

Days and weeks passed and no word from anyone. Was Mother on her way to Drancy, the camp Mr. Broca mentioned when referring to Papa? (Drancy was a camp near Paris where deportees were being assembled before being sent to Auschwitz.)

Was I ever going to see her again? And what about Opa? Where was he? And what about my father? I found it hard to concentrate. I couldn't play chess with Henri and felt bad that I was spoiling his fun. But he seemed to understand and was supportive: "Don't worry, George, they'll be okay. You just have to be patient."

* * *

Six weeks had passed, and I began to lose hope of seeing Mother and Grandfather ever again. No word from Father either. Then, one afternoon, the telephone rang.

"It's your mother, George. Quick, run to the phone!" said Mrs. Waisblatt.

"Hi, Mother, are you all right?"

"I am fine, my darling, not to worry. I'll explain everything later. Just come home," Mother said in a strange voice.

"Yes, Mother. I'm so happy to hear you're all right. I'll be there."

I thanked Henri's parents for saving me. They gave me a big hug, and I left within minutes. They gave me money for the streetcar, and Henri's mother told me to be very careful.

As I prepared to leave, I thought that Mother's voice had sounded unusually high pitched. Was she speaking freely? Was anyone there telling her to call me? Did she have a gun pointed at her, forcing her to say the correct thing to me? Was this the trap that would clinch my arrest?

My imagination was running wild. I felt as if I was playing a part in a gangster movie, but had forgotten my lines and I couldn't remember how the plot was supposed to end.

'Just come home' Mother had said. No admonitions or warning to be careful, which I thought was unusual.

The rush hour had passed and the city was getting ready to settle down for the night. The street lights had just come on. Cars were turning on their headlights and shopkeepers were pulling down their roller gates.

As I neared home, I wondered about what Henri's mother had said. Should I approach the house carefully? Not just walk in, as if nothing had happened: What if it was a trap? I should be prepared to run again as fast as I could. I finally concluded that I would act the way Humphrey Bogart would act in a similar situation.

I sneaked around to the back of the house, and like a private eye, tried to evaluate the risks involved in breaking in. Lights were on, shutters were open, but curtains were drawn. Through a window on the second floor, I saw a woman walking across the room. It looked like Mother, but I couldn't be sure. Was there someone else in the room with her? Through the curtains I saw a shadow move back and forth but couldn't identify whether it was Mother's or someone else's.

I decided to wait outside for a while before taking the risk of falling into a possible trap. After an hour, I saw a woman again, and this time, I was sure it was Mother. She didn't appear to be in any distress, but seemed to be waiting impatiently and pacing the floor.

I decided to take my chances and enter the house through the back porch. Mother was waiting in the living room.

"What took you so long? I thought something had happened to you since we talked on the phone three hours ago."

"Mother, I'll explain everything after you tell me what happened to you."

* * *

Mother was happy to see me. It seemed like our lives were being fractured since my childhood, and that being reunited was a recurring event in our relationship.

'Is there any relationship that is closer and stronger than the one between mother and son?' I thought. I knew that for Mother, the answer to that question was an absolute "no." Her love for me was totally unconditional, and I felt it deep in my heart. I couldn't wait to hear the story of her ordeal.

"Tell me all about what happened to you?" I asked.

"Well, the Police came with a warrant. They took me to Police Headquarters and started questioning me. They wanted to know if we were involved with the FFI (Free French forces) or the Resistance. And they wanted to know all about my husband? And why did the Gestapo know about us?"

"So, what did you say?"

"I tried to gain time," she said. "I remembered that I knew the Associate Chief of Police, Mr. Jacques Soustelle. You remember he had been a good customer in our restaurant, and we had become friends after a while. I had not seen him for a long time. So, I inquired about him."

After a pause, she took a deep breath and went on. "They seemed surprised that I knew Jacques Soustelle. But they wondered what connection I had with such a high official. When I told them he was a steady customer at my restaurant and a good friend, they finally consented to inform him that I was being detained under suspicion of subversive activity and of being Jewish. I swore to them that I wasn't Jewish, showed them my cross, and that I had nothing to do with the Resistance."

"Did they believe you?" I asked.

"They put me in a cell, gave me some clear soup, and told me that it would be a few days before they got in touch with Mr. Soustelle. I felt that I had only one chance: that he would still like me and that he would intervene."

She took a sip of tea and after I checked the door, she went on. "Interrogations continued for several days. I kept repeating my explanations that some jealous and resentful neighbors had lied about our listening to the BBC, and that we were not Jewish, that my husband and I had been good Catholics."

I could sense that Mother was getting tired, but she continued.

"Mother, why don't you rest for a while. You'll finish later," I said.

"No, darling. I want you to know what happened."

"All right, but then you must promise me that you'll rest."

"The interrogations began to wear me down. They threatened to send me away, to beat me, to arrest the rest of the family. Although I didn't know of your whereabouts, I was afraid that they would find you."

She continued her story. "No word from Jacques Soustelle. I was losing hope. Then, I decided to play a wild card. I said that I was of German descent and I asked to speak to the local German or SS Commander, and hoped that they wouldn't trace me to our prior German contacts in Bordeaux."

"How did you manage in the cell?" I asked.

"It was horrible, George. Cockroaches everywhere. A pail for a toilet. Straw on the floor for the bed. No towels. No place to sit. No heat. Mice and rats at night. A real hell."

I felt a chill all over. I was amazed that Mother could endure such ignominious treatment at the hands of these barbarians.

I shuddered and looked around and wondered if we were being watched. I put myself on high alert, but didn't say anything to Mother.

She took another sip of tea and hugged me. "I'm so happy you're all right. I couldn't stand the thought if something happened to you."

"So, tell me how it ended?" I asked.

"They continued to harass me for three weeks. Finally, on the fifth week, they brought in a German officer to interrogate me in German."

She paused, and drank more tea.

"I spoke my best 'hoch Deutsch' with him. I explained that I had been framed by jealous French people who didn't like my German descent. I don't know if he believed me, but I think he liked me."

I was afraid to ask Mother what she meant by that and if more had taken place between her and the German officer. Frankly, I didn't want to know.

"On the sixth week, one morning, I was released and given tram fare home."

I hugged her hard and held back my tears for fear of upsetting her.

* * *

A week later Father called. He had gotten word from his landlady not to return to his apartment. After staying with friends for a couple of weeks, he had relocated in another apartment near the Rhone river.

Now, he was acting the role of undercover agent I had attributed to him when we had our first meeting. He got new identity papers, a new fictitious name (Berteau, which sounded very French), a new

197

trench coat, and kept his trademark of a lit cigarette hanging out the side of his mouth.

I listened on the other phone line.

"I think we should stay apart for a while," he said to Mother," at least until things calm down a bit."

"Yes, we need to be sure they won't pick up a trail," said Mother.

"Best is for you to call my friend, Samuel, in a few weeks when you think the coast is clear," he said.

"Is George all right. I heard he had to run away from my apartment."

I chimed in. "Yes, Father, I'm all right. I got away thanks to Mrs. Bourdier, the landlady."

"Yeah, she saved my life too," he said, "and we must be careful from now on just in case we're being watched."

Mother agreed to the new plan of staying away from each other, at least for awhile.

She ended the conversation. "All right. But we'll miss you, dear. Good bye."

* * *

Grandfather had been missing for several weeks. Mother said she didn't dare call her friend, Jacques Soustelle, the Associate Chief of Police, to find out what had happened to Opa.

After all, Soustelle had not intervened for her when she was in jail. Why should she expect anything from him now?

She also said that she didn't want to arouse further suspicion and push her luck. So we agreed to wait and hope for the best.

I knew that Opa had been arrested when my father's landlady told me as I came to the apartment. But was he still alive after that much time without his heart medicine? Without proper food?

After all, he was in his seventies, getting frail and helpless. What could they possibly want from an old man, anyway?

As we were settling down to do some reading after dinner, the restaurant had been closed for renovations, we heard a knock on the door. Mother looked at me, wondering what to do. Should we ignore it? Could it be the Police again? I winked at her and tiptoed to the door.

On the door step, was a sight I'll never forget. An old man was standing in the doorway. He was bent over, had blood on his face and hands, and was black and blue all over. He was wearing tattered clothes, was barefoot and barely able to speak,

"Oh! My God, Opa. What in the world happened to you? Come in."

I helped him through the door when he shuffled in. He was in a great deal of pain. Choked by her emotions, Mother rushed to the door, held him and helped him sit down on the sofa.

"George, get some gauze and warm water. Quick," she yelled out "Also, get some custard, bread and warm soup from the kitchen."

I rushed to the kitchen, feeling sick to my stomach from the cruel sight of my poor grandfather. How could they have done this to him?

I swore to myself that I would seek revenge some day. But inside, I was raging against the people who must have reported us to the Gestapo. Maybe these people who squealed on us were collaborators hoping to get a nice reward for their information.

There was no way to know who was and who wasn't a collaborator. One always had to be suspicious and on guard for fear of making a mistake that might cost one's life.

It took days for Opa to recover from his ordeal. He was reluctant to talk about it, but bits and pieces of the story came out as the weeks went by.

It looked as though he had been picked up at my father's apartment where he had been waiting for me.

When they found the material I had written, it was so incriminating that he was immediately arrested and taken to jail. But was it the same jail where Mother had been incarcerated, or was it the famous Montluc jail where they kept hard-core criminals and hostages? He couldn't say.

In his case, knowing German didn't seem to have helped. Both French and German interrogators pounded their fists on his face, his body and limbs, totally unconcerned about his age.

They wanted him to tell where the anti-Nazi poems came from. Who wrote them? Was there a nest of Resistance fighters behind these pieces of writing?

They continued to beat him to make him talk, but he kept resisting, swearing that he had no knowledge of this material, its content or its source. He told them that he didn't know how it had gotten into the apartment. He insisted, in German, that he was visiting an old friend and didn't know anything about his activities. When asked about my father and me, he said that he didn't know of our whereabouts and that he was living with my mother—which was how they eventually got to her.

They robbed him of his gold watch and denied him the nitroglycerine which kept his angina in check. Now, his excruciating chest pain was adding to the pounding fists during the interrogations.

I don't know how he survived this ordeal: An old man, receiving no medical care, no food, no hygiene, just daily beatings. It was beyond me to imagine anyone surviving these conditions, let alone poor Opa.

One day, without any explanation, they put him in a car and took him to an isolated road in the countryside outside Lyon. They threw him in a ditch and drove away. Despite severe chest pain and bleeding from his wounds, he walked slowly back to the city, across town and back to our house.

He had survived WWI as a young man. But I wondered if, as an old man, he would survive this ugly war?

19- The Bomb Shelter

While we resumed life with renewed hope, battles were being fought on many fronts all over the world. News filtered to us through the Nazi propaganda broadcasts that we interpreted by reading it between the lines and by comparing it to the news from the BBC.

By 1941, the German army was fighting on Russian soil. Could they ever be stopped? The Vichy propaganda declared them victorious every day. Several German panzer divisions had broken through the Russian lines on the north and south of Moscow. However, news from the BBC in late October and early November gave a different story.

The sudden onset of cold weather had thrown a damper on the German advance. The cold had frozen engine oil, packing grease and firing mechanisms. German troops did not have winter uniforms and they were falling victim to frostbite. Their morale was sinking quickly. By December 6th, Zhukov, the Russian general, had led a decisive counter-attack. The German army had already suffered over

155,000 casualties and had been pushed back as far back as 40 miles from Moscow. Hitler had shifted his forces into another direction.

The French radio announced that the German troops were concentrating their efforts in the southern part of the Caucasus. They reported that General Paulus, the newly appointed German commander of the 6th Army would attack Stalingrad with the help of the 4th Panzer Army. Within a few days they reached the outskirts of Stalingrad.

According to the German propaganda, the German Army was fighting in the streets of Stalingrad.

We listened to the French radio and to the BBC. Our morale would ebb and flow with the latest communiqués.

Would Russia have to surrender? Was this going to be the end of Russia and perhaps the end the world?

On the sixth of November, the Germans were halted in the Caucasus. In the thick of winter, the frozen and mauled German Sixth Army under General Von Paulus was encircled. The Luftwaffe had been unable to supply the army from the air. German soldiers were dying in droves under the brutal frost.

Just like their Holocaust victims had had to endure, now the Germans had to hide in rat-infested holes while lice fed on their emaciated bodies. On the nineteenth, the Soviets launched a massive counter-offensive on the Central Front and on the twentyninth, another one in the Caucasus.

Finally, the Germans withdrew on the 2nd of January, 1943, and General Paulus, commander of the German 6th Army, surrendered at Stalingrad on February 2nd.

The final count: 240,000 German troops dead and 94,000 prisoners of war taken by the Russians. On the Russian side: 253,000 perished from December to February. The Battle of Stalingrad had been so important to Stalin and Hitler that they had expended the lives of more than half a million people in just five months.

The Battle of Stalingrad was one of the most significant turning points in the war. For the first time, since Hitler had marched into all of Europe, the gigantic Nazi war machine had been stopped by the massive Soviet counteroffensive. When we heard this news on the BBC, we all cheered and we began to have hopes again.

On another front the Germans were defeated in Africa and had to retreat to Italy. The BBC announced that the Italian government changed its allegiance and joined the Allies. In July, 1943, the news came that Mussolini was arrested by the new Italian government of Badoglio but shortly afterwards was freed by German paratroopers and abducted to Germany.

* * *

For weeks, we had been listening to the usual cryptic messages on the BBC: "The rats are leaving the pastures", "The bulls are smiling at the moon."

We speculated that big things were going to happen soon but didn't know exactly what. We heard that the Wehrmacht was losing ground in Russia, while Hamburg, Dresden and Cologne were virtually destroyed.

Berlin, too, was heavily damaged. French cities were being bombed by the Americans now. Strangely enough, Paris was not bombed by the Germans, the British or the Americans. But Lyon was a likely target because of its heavy concentrations of troops, its main railroad networks and suspected large arsenals.

Mother said it was wise to abandon the restaurant as it was probably being watched by the French police as a place suspected of subversive activities. Without delay we packed our things, and Mother, Opa and I moved to a new apartment on the quai Fulchiron bordering the river Saone near the passerelle St George, a walking bridge. We agreed that this was a good place to hide. No one in that neighborhood knew who we were. Eventually, Mother bought the restaurant under the apartment.

My father had been tipped off by his landlady during the raid of his apartment and had not returned but had relocated in another apartment a few blocs away from our new residence.

Like everyone else in the building, we obeyed the rules about the air raid drills which required our going to the nearest shelter as soon as the sirens would start wailing.

On May 26, 1944, a clear and sunny morning, we heard the deafening wailing of the sirens.

We got out of bed, washed in a hurry, put a few clothes on, and rushed down the stairs. I shouted to Mother, "I'm going to look at those American B-17s. See you later."

"No, George. You're going to the shelter. Please, remember you promised!"

"I'll see you there in a short while. I just want to see those damn planes."

"All right then. Don't be long," she said.

I rushed down to the lobby and to the front of the building.

High in the sky, like swarms of honeybees, hundreds of planes were droning overhead.

The entire sky was blanketed with small dark dots moving in an orderly fashion. What an incredible sight! The air was filled with the sounds of whirring engines, and I had the feeling that something big was going to happen.

Anti-aircraft guns started shooting, and I could see the puffs of black smoke peppering the sky.

I was mesmerized by this show of modern warfare, but remembered my promise to Mother about going to the shelter two blocks away.

I heard a huge explosion and felt my body being lifted into the air and then, miraculously, I landed on the bank of the river. Confused, disheveled, my eardrums still popping, I got up and started walking, wondering where the shelter was. My knees were bleeding, but since I could walk, I didn't think my legs were broken.

Black smoke was enveloping the street above the embankment. Buildings were ablaze. No firemen were in sight. I kept walking, dazed and bewildered, coughing from the thick black smoke around me.

Bodies were lying everywhere, some dead others bleeding. A woman's skull had been cut open and was still barely attached to the body. A boy was bleeding next to his severed arm. Other people were searching blindly for relatives everywhere in the rubble. Broken glass littered the ground. Moans and screams could be heard all over. An acid smell like ammonia was floating in the air all over the neighborhood.

Then I remembered. Oh, my God, where was Mother? Did she go to the shelter? What about Opa?

I approached an old man sitting by a lamp post, "Do you know which way is the shelter?" He looked at me, haggard and staring me in the face, he said. "Don't go there, son. The shelter. It's gone. It was a direct hit. Just like that walking bridge, the St Georges, you see over there. It's gone too."

My brain started to short-circuit. Mother and Opa, where were they? Did she go to the shelter as she said she would? Is she hurt?' I must find her. I can't stand the thought of it. I don't care what the man said. I thought that I must check out the apartment across the street.

I looked up. I could see the inside of the building and into all the apartments, as the face of the building had been literally shaved off. I ran into the lobby. The stairs were gone. I went back into the street.

I could see the second floor. People were screaming and calling, "Jo, Charles, Francoise, Alice, Serge, Antoine, where are you? Please, answer. Please, for God's sake, answer me."

Out of the cacophony, I heard a voice calling "George, George, George, where are you?"

On the second floor, standing on the edge, was Mother, her dress in shreds, her face and hair blackened by the smoke, yelling my name with a desperate scream, "George, George, answer me?"

"I'm here, Mother. Look over here. Downstairs in the street."

A man brought a ladder, and with his help, she came down. She grabbed me and held me tight in her arms, saying, "Oh, my God! Oh, my God! You are all right. Aren't you?"

"Yes, Mother. I'm fine. Where's Opa?"

We found him in a pile of rubble. He was covered with soot. He smiled as soon as he saw us.

Amid clouds of black smoke and burning fires, we walked away, holding each other, in search of another place to live. Once more, I thanked Providence for being kind to all three of us.

* * *

Next day's headlines reported the casualties: Over 1500 dead, several hundred critically wounded, many shell-shocked, others simply homeless and destitute. This was one of the worst air raids in the city of Lyon. The major industrial center destroyed. A few stray bombs killing civilians and hitting a few bridges. One of the bridges was a walking bridge—the St Georges across from our apartment on the Saone.

One shelter had suffered a direct hit, killing two hundred people. I knew the shelter they were talking about, the one that we were supposed to have gone to.

*   *   *

As I am writing this on September 12, 2001, I read in this morning's headlines:

"World Trade Towers and Pentagon Hit by Terrorists. Thousands civilians killed. Hundreds critically wounded. Thousands homeless and destitute." Different place. Different times. Same effect. Same result. Death and devastation. Raw hatred ruling men in blind rage.

Will the carnage ever stop? After the holocaust, the phrase "Never Again" was reverberating throughout the world.

Last year in Kosovo, we were talking about "ethnic cleansing", a new euphemism for the elimination of an entire people. This year the Taliban talks about "religious cleansing." They arrested a handful of Americans, accused of preaching Christianity. They are requiring Hindus to wear a strip of yellow cloth to be sewn onto a shirt pocket in order to identify themselves. Is this the equivalent of the yellow star Jews were compelled to wear in WWII?

Again, nations are debating who should intervene? Whose problem is it? How much money, weapons, arms, soldiers can we spare? Why can't diplomacy resolve this problem? Is this just a U.S. problem or a concern for the entire free world? Why can't the UN reach a consensus on this horrible devastation?

This year the West is uniting against a new enemy called "terrorism." The main suspect is Osama bin Laden, but there are thousands of bin Ladens in many countries. This will be a long and protracted war President Bush says.

While the world is arguing over these questions, people are dying by the thousands, as they did in WWII, Korea, Vietnam, Somalia, Iraq, Rwanda, Chechnya, Kosovo, Israel and the United States.

Why can't we all get along? Will the religious wars in Ireland, Middle East, Europe, Asia ever end?

Is fighting and killing the only answer to being different, to feeling inferior or alienated, to wanting domination over others? Questions, questions and more questions, but no real answers! Problems, but no real solutions!

I think that as long as leaders addicted to power will threaten and oppress the weak and helpless, there will be wars, devastation, and cruelty by men to other men.

20- Barbie and Touviers

It was not until years later and many recurrent dreams that I realized how close my family and I had come to perishing in the web of the German and French police, which consisted of reprisals, raids and random executions.

By June 1941, life had become more complicated all over France.

The French Resistance fighters, Communists and Gaullist, started committing many acts of sabotage and carrying out assassinations of Germans.

An Army major and a government official were shot in Bordeaux. Another high ranking officer, the Field Commander of Nantes, was shot on October 20, 1941.

The reprisals that followed were ferocious. By October 25, over a hundred hostages, taken from political prisoners, Communists, and Jews were executed. Fifty five were from Bordeaux, 48 from Nantes and the rest from little towns in between.

The bodies of hostages were often displayed on major intersections for the population to see and be reminded of the grim reprisals for attacks against Germans.

I shuddered as I walked by these poor souls sprawled on the curb in torn and bloody clothes and wondered if I knew any of them. I didn't have the courage to get close enough to find out. Besides, there were guards who might become suspicious, if I dared.

There were more assassinations of German soldiers carried out by the Resistance. The price to pay, however, was high. Newspapers would report the assassinations and the reprisals to alert and warn the population at large. News traveled by word of mouth and underground newspapers that reported more accurately the arrests of dissidents and Jews.

German reprisals with the cooperation of French Police focused primarily on Jews. In May 1941, they arrested and interned 3600 Polish Jews around Paris and in August they arrested another group.

Towards the end of 1941, one thousand Jewish notables had been arrested, and a fine of a billion francs was imposed on the Jewish population of the entire Occupied Zone.

In May and June of 1942 the mass deportation of Jews in the Occupied Zone began. These Jews had been required to wear the yellow star of David after May 28, 1942.

In the Unoccupied Zone, only Jewish registration with the police was required. It was a little known fact that Petain had requested that Jews in the Unoccupied Zone be spared the burden of wearing a yellow star, and even after November 1942, when all of France became occupied the yellow star was optional.

Mother and I agreed to abstain from such registration while several of my friends chose to comply. But we always lived under the threat that someone might report us to the police even though Mother wore a golden cross quite prominently.

Himmler had set definite quotas for the extermination of Jews at Auschwitz. He had earmarked 15,000 from Holland, 10,000 from Belgium and 100,000 from France, half from the Unoccupied Zone.

Of an estimated 300,000 to 350,000 French Jews, about 85,000 were deported. Years later, I read that 6,000 French Jews had taken the gruesome journey to Auschwitz.

About one million people were exterminated in Auschwitz, mostly Jews but also Poles, Russian prisoners-of-war and Gypsies.

During the period between May and July 1944, 400,000 Hungarian Jews were deported and killed there. Pravda newspaper reported that 'three to five railway carriages packed with people arrived daily at the camp, and 10,000 to 12,000 persons were killed daily in death chambers.'

As we learned in 1945, in a letter from the Red Cross, one of the Jews was my father (Papa), who was taken to Auschwitz on the 23rd of June, 1943 and did not survive.

For years I hoped that the Red Cross had made a mistake and that another letter would come, apologizing for their error. My belief grew stronger after I learned that almost 3,000 French Jews had survived the ordeal. But as the years passed, I came to accept the inevitable truth that his disappearance was permanent.

Klaus Barbie, Chief of the Gestapo in Lyon, carried out the mission of rounding up Resistance fighters and Jews with a zeal that exceeded that shown by his French counterpart, the milice man Paul Touviers.

When Mother and Opa were arrested under the Barbie and Touviers regime, there wasn't much anyone could have done. In retrospect, Mother's account of her arrest, interrogation, and treatment in jail suggested to me that she had been dealing with Barbie's men. Ironically, an SS man whose authority superseded the Milice eventually released her.

On the other hand, the way that Opa had been manhandled indicated to me that he had been in the grips of the Milice under Touviers who acted more like highway robbers than Gestapo men.

Even Marshal Petain was shocked at the treatment French Jews received and, in a gesture of protest against the Germans, presented himself as a hostage at the Demarcation Line on October 25th. Further executions were temporarily stopped, but Vichy, under intense pressure to put a stop to terrorism by the Resistance, was helpless in stopping the carnage on both sides.

* * *

The Germans had first occupied Lyon in June 1940, but following the terms of the armistice, retreated to what was to be known as the Occupied Zone.

In November 1942, after the Allied forces had landed in North Africa, the Germans re-occupied the rest of France. They established Gestapo headquarters in all the major cities and continued spreading fear and intimidation everywhere.

Jews, Communists and French Resistance fighters were primary targets while local folks who offered to turn them in to the authorities would receive substantial monetary rewards. No one knew who were the collaborators or who believed in or worked for the Resistance.

The French police would make what was called "rafles de Juifs", which meant the rounding up of Jews to be sent to Drancy, the center for deportation to concentration camps.

After the Germans reoccupied the city of Lyon in November 1942, the policy for capturing Jews and Resisters continued with an even greater and vicious zeal than ever before.

The man in Lyon who promoted this policy of ruling through fear was Klaus Barbie, known as the butcher of Lyon. Barbie was chief of

Section IV of the Sipo-SD in Lyon, an administrative branch of the SS specially assigned to track down members of the Resistance and to organize the Final Solution against the Jews in the region of Lyon.

Barbie was the man who was responsible for torturing and executing Jean Moulin, the envoy that De Gaulle had sent to France to organize and lead the Resistance.[1]

As I write this, I am shocked to discover that a 10,000 page document, declassified by the CIA mentioned that 20 Nazi criminals had been working as intelligence sources for the U.S. Army's Counterintelligence Corps or the Office of Strategic Services, a forerunner of the CIA, during the Cold War between East and West. Klaus Barbie had been one of the agents working as a counterintelligence source and therefore was not pursued as a war criminal.[1]

In 1987, Barbie was arrested by the French police in Guyana and indicted for crimes against humanity in Lyon. He was condemned for

---

[1]The document, released by the CIA, revealed that 20 Nazi figures had escaped justice after the war because the West valued them as Cold War intelligence sources, according to Eli Rosenbaum of the Justice Department's Nazi-hunting Office of Special Investigations. Among them were Klaus Barbie, Security Police member Emil Augsburg and SS Officer Wilhelm Hoetll. Officials noted that Britain, France, West Germany and the Soviet Union also embraced war criminals. (The Desert Sun, April 28, 2001.)

having deported forty-four Jewish children from Izieu. He said that he had rounded as many Jews as he could that day in order to "carry out the policy of systematic extermination, a policy created by the highest level of the Reich command." He was sentenced to a life term and died in prison in September 1991. The lengthy trial was filmed and televised to a large French audience for 70 hours out of 185 hours of trial.

*   *   *

Barbie had been assisted by Paul Touviers, Chief of the Milice in Lyon. People shuddered just at the sound of his name.

The Milice, a French arm of the Gestapo, was everywhere, and one couldn't tell them apart from other French people. They were dressed in civilian clothes and looked like anyone else in the community. When one spoke to strangers, one didn't know if they were part of the Milice or not. One didn't know who was trustworthy, who was resentful, or who was a collaborator. One had to be suspicious of everyone to survive in this environment.

Touviers' Milice was made up primarily of criminal elements who were more interested in plundering and pillaging the apartments of Jews than in exhaustively tracking down their victims. That task was more effectively and passionately done by the SS. The regular Vichy French police were more murderous in following Bousquet's anti-Jewish policy to the letter (Bousquet was a high ranking French official in the Vichy government in charge of the deportation of French Jews.)

Touviers was a faithful assistant to Barbie, operating in the same general location of Lyon and its outlying areas.

On June 28, 1944, three members of the Resistance, disguised as members of the Milice, shot and killed Vichy's propaganda minister, Philippe Henriot at his residence in Paris.

In immediate reprisals, seven Frenchmen were executed in their homes in Macon. Other reprisals followed in Toulouse, Clermont-Ferrant, Grenoble and Voiron.

In Lyon, Paul Touviers ordered the rounding up of seven more hostages and the arrest of a large number of Jews. On his order, seven

Jews were taken to the cemetery at Rillieux-la-Pape, stood against a wall, and executed at dawn.

Years later I learned that it took forty years for Touviers, the Milice Chief, who had been responsible for my mother's and grandfather's arrests, to be charged and convicted of crimes against humanity.

Touviers was a complex personality, able to dupe and con members of the Catholic Church, whose role during the war years, was highly dubious and ambiguous. Catholic clergy believed that Touviers himself was being persecuted by post-war authorities, and they saw him as a modern day Christian martyr! While Bousquet was able to obtain the protection of other government post-war officials, Touviers was able to get the support of the Catholic Church. The latter provided him with shelter and money for many years.

Others in the media saw his redeeming virtues, including the famed singer Jacques Brel and the philosopher Gabriel Marcel.

Writing about himself in his book "Mes Crimes contre l'humanité" (My Crimes Against Humanity), Touviers compared himself to Saint Paul, offering the so-called "Schindler defense" later used during his trial. He claimed that in the face of tremendous pressures from the Germans and French superiors, he was able "to reduce greatly the number of Jewish victims at Rillieux-la-Pape in 1944.

In reality, Touviers had been known as the "executioner of Lyon." Even de Gaulle said unequivocally that Touviers was fully deserving of the firing squad.

Touviers joined the Vichy government at its beginning, and eventually enlisted in the Service d'Ordre Legionnaire (SOL), which became the Milice in January 1943.

The Milice was the alternative offered to Frenchmen who did not want to volunteer for the labor force in Germany. After his enlistment Touviers rose through the ranks of the Milice and was named Head for the entire Rhone region.

He became a significant force within and outside the Milice. He confiscated the apartment of a Jewish textile industrialist and, in a gangster-like fashion, started a career of plundering Jewish victims, confiscating apartments, cars, jewels, furniture, and money, for which he was never charged in his trial.

He was charged, however, with treason and sentenced to death in absentia first in Lyon in 1946 and later again in Chambery in 1947. Often rescued by friendly priests, Touviers spent most of the post-war years in hiding and on the run, but was finally arrested in Nice in 1989.

Once in custody, a lengthy and controversial investigation was launched against Touviers. The Court did not deem it necessary to keep him in prison in order to "uncover the truth." Touviers was suffering from prostate cancer, although without any effect.

The Court showed compassion toward Touviers and disregarded the history of total brutality he had exerted towards his victims. The Catholic Church secured him a Presidential pardon from Georges Pompidou. Public outrage was intense although short-lived.

The French press and the justices in the French judiciary had spent years debating the merits of the case. Why did it take so long?

Why couldn't the French see that crimes against humanity or war crimes deserved to be punished? Why should there be a statute of limitation? Why should legal technicalities apply when proof of cruelty and brutality were involved? Why should following orders be an excuse for murdering and brutalizing innocent people? Why should swearing an oath of loyalty to Hitler be a valid excuse? Why should preserving "French unity" be a reasonable explanation? Why should preserving French purity against Jewish "leprosy" be a valid ideology? Why shouldn't Darnand who was the real Chief, the secretary general of the Milice and a member of the Waffen SS as well, be held responsible for these acts of cruelty and murder? Why couldn't the French see all of this?

* * *

In its analysis, the French Court found that Vichy had not officially made statements against the Jews. But not even the Jewish Statute, the Yellow Star, nor the texts of Vichy excluding the Jews from normal participation in community life, nor the organized arrests, the massacres—including the ones ordered by Touviers— were sufficient proof that these amounted to an "official proclamation" of anti-Semitism!

With this reasoning, the French High Court decided to acquit Paul Touviers in April 1992, basing their decision on the fact that Touviers had acted on behalf of the French Vichy regime and therefore his actions could only be classified as "war crimes" rather than crimes against humanity. And because the statute of limitations against war crimes had long since gone into effect, he could not be held responsible!

But even though French government officials admitted that the decision by the highest court in the land had been "a terrible decision", the wheels of justice had spun, and nothing more could be done to reverse the decision.

For years, Mother and Opa's arrests and my own narrow escape from the Touviers and Barbie men had triggered dozens of recurring nightmares which never led to a resolution except for sudden awakening in cold sweat. Only the fading of aging memory seems to have diminished the pain from those nightmares.

Have we not experienced many times in history the fact that the victims of atrocities and war crimes are often the last to get justice and acknowledgment of their suffering?

Will this be the last time we hear of a High Court exonerating high ranking killers charged with "crimes against humanity"? I don't think so.

21- The Resistance

I learned first hand about the Resistance when Uncle David confided to me that he had a big part in it. He offered no details, and I knew better than pry for classified information.

Years later, I learned that starting a program of resistance had not come easily in France. First, it had been extremely risky to go against the law, and only the young, the Communists and the already outcast street fighters would consider such a move. Germans had labeled sabotage resistance fighters as Communists and had executed them on the spot.

From 1940 on, small groups of Frenchmen began to organize pockets of resistance manned mostly with Communists and Gaullists.

The region of Lyon and its surroundings became the main center of the Resistance movement with its three distinct groups under the name of "Combat", "Liberation" and "Franc-Tireur. They functioned as separate entities and proudly guarded their independence, while exercising a certain amount of rivalry between them. Initially, their goal was to defeat and frustrate the Vichy government operations, but as time went on, they developed military plans to attack the German army of occupation. Their problem was that they had no arms, no ammunitions, no explosives and no communication equipment.

De Gaulle realized that there was an urgent need to organize and unify these new and isolated guerrilla forces made up of thousands of young men ready and able to fight the enemy from within.

As Chief of Free France, he wanted to assume command of this significant force and to convince the Allies that this force was reliable, dependable and significant, and therefore needed to be supplied with military equipment.

To achieve this goal, he asked Jean Moulin, the former Chartres prefect and a man with strong leadership qualities, to unify all the isolated groups and persuade them to accept de Gaulle as their leader.

On the night of January 1, 1942, Jean Moulin parachuted to the south of France to get the three respective chiefs of the local resistance Henry Frenay, Emmanuel d'Astier de la Vigerie, and Jean-Pierre Levy to agree to unite and give up their proud independence. In exchange, he promised to give them full support from de Gaulle, coordination with the Allied Forces and the supply of military equipment. Furthermore, he offered to provide an effective administrative structure that would unify, solidify, merge and streamline all their services.

After a series of long negotiations, he succeeded in convincing the chiefs that the unification and consolidation of their efforts would result in a much more efficient force.

By the end of the summer of 1942, these chiefs were willing to accept de Gaulle as their Commander in Chief, and his designate, General Delestraint, as the commander of the new paramilitary force and the new Secret Army (A.S.)

The consolidation was finalized in January 1943, under the new name of "United Movements of the Resistance", known under the initials M.U.R. Other small splinter groups continued to exist, especially one led by the Communist Party.

In May 1943, Jean Moulin brought all the various factions together and, as de Gaulle had hoped, he was elected Chairman of the "National Council of the Resistance for all of France."

A clandestine press was established in Lyon and played a significant role in coordinating passive resistance in the community.

George M. Burnell, M.D.

When the German command ordered French young men to report for work in German factories, the underground papers called for major strikes. As these strikes went into effect they successfully paralyzed services in the whole region.

When Jews were persecuted and arrested in mass to be deported, the secret press appealed to citizens to revolt against these atrocities. One such operation succeeded in the summer of 1942, when 108 Jewish children and a handful of adults were surreptitiously diverted and hidden from the Gestapo.

The Resistance began to be an effective force to be reckoned with, and Germans could no longer ignore it. They decided to take several steps to counteract this annoying sting operation.

First, Hitler started to put pressure on the Vichy government to recruit young men who would be willing to fight the resistance guerrillas and help out the French Police.

Pierre Laval, the head of the Vichy government, came up with a clever scheme. He enacted a law that gave young men between the ages of 18 to 25 a choice of going to serve in German arms factories or to join a paramilitary police force called the Milice. Armed by the

SS and styled after the Gestapo, it specialized in capturing and torturing resistance fighters.

Several thousand young men chose to flee in the hills and join the resistance fighters. Nearly 700,000 Frenchmen reported for so-called STO (Service du Travail Obligatoire), the Obligatory Work Service. Under the program, men between sixteen and sixty years of age would be ordered—not asked—to go to Germany.

Anyone who resisted or tried to escape would be hunted down and punished severely. To back up his threat, Laval relied on the Milice men for reprisals.

A contingent of 45,000 ruthless men volunteered to join the Milice. They were given free rein to pursue their cruel and sadistic outlet for chasing Jews, Communists and their former buddies who had chosen to be Resistance fighters and had joined the guerrilla forces known as the *"Maquis"* (French for *woods*) in the hills.

The Milice became dreaded as much as the Gestapo itself. Their methods were the same and consisted of plundering, pillaging, torturing and executing thousands of people arrested under the charge of being Jewish, Communist or resistance fighters. Anyone could be charged, based on a suspicion by a neighbor, or on a quick on-the-spot evaluation by a Milice man. No one was safe or beyond suspicion. Seeing these Frenchmen dressed in khaki shirts, black berets and black ties inspired fear and hatred throughout the population.

As the Resistance fighters learned to deal with the Milice, another development made life more complicated.

In November 1942, Hitler decided to take another step. He became concerned about the Allies, who had landed in Morocco and Algiers.

To counteract this momentous move, he ordered the Wehrmacht to eliminate the Demarcation Line and to invade the rest of France.

Now, Resistance fighters had to confront not only the Milice but German troops everywhere. Suddenly they had to conceal their lines of communication and their secret radio emitting stations that coordinated sabotage operations. Parachuted drops of arms from the Allies were more difficult to plan ahead and to conceal from the enemy. In addition, resistance fighters had to worry about potential collaborators among their midst.

Everyone knew that a significant portion of the population and businesses collaborated with the Germans. These collaborators provided information about resistance fighters, the location of Jews, and tips of secret meetings and planned sabotage operations announced in underground newspapers. In exchange for the collaborators' help, the Germans offered them monetary rewards, food, medication and much needed equipment.

In June of 1943, the Gestapo arrested masses of people accused of being connected with subversive activities, many who were denounced by collaborators.

On the 9th of June, General Delestraint, the Chief of the newly formed Secret Army in charge of the resistance intelligence networks, was arrested in Paris.

On June 21st, Jean Moulin, the man who had been the key to unifying all the Resistance groups, was captured by the Gestapo in Caluire, a suburb of Lyon. He, along with several members of his military command, had been denounced to the authorities by a traitor in their midst. This was a tremendous setback for the resistance fighters all over France.

Whenever members of the French Resistance were captured, they were first tortured, and then either sent before a firing squad or deported to die a lingering death in German concentration camps. Moulin was tortured by the infamous Klaus Barbie and died during his transfer to Germany.

An estimate after the war showed that 400,000 Frenchmen had served officially in the Resistance (about 2 percent of the adult French population.) Those were the men who, after the war, were given official veteran status by the Liberation government of de Gaulle.

Among them, 100,000 died in active service, 130,000 were deported, and 170,000 of them received official honors for their bravery and loyalty.

One of them who was granted such high honors was my Uncle David.

22- Bourgoin and Jallieu

Uncle David had always been a proud man. He had practiced dentistry in Paris and had taught at the School of Dentistry of the University of Paris. At the onset of the war when Jews were barred from practicing, he had closed his office and moved his family into the Unoccupied Zone. After a short stay in Toulouse, he, Aunt Ethel and Cousin Betty came to Grenoble. A few months later they moved again. They settled in a small community called Bourgoin-Jallieu in the summer of 1942. It was a quaint village populated by many generations of French people whose ancestors went back to the Middle Ages. Newcomers were few and far between, but Uncle David was immediately welcomed because the people were happy to have a dentist in the area for the first time.

Since Mother and I had moved away from Grenoble, I had missed Uncle David. I looked up to him as a new father figure. He was strong, articulate, and spoke with a voice that would have melted an iceberg. He was tall, had an athletic build, dark thin hair and deep brown eyes that could smile, or disapprove if one were doing something wrong or nasty.

In his presence, one could sense immediately an aura of leadership as he spoke, proudly standing erect, looking one straight in the eyes.

I felt privileged to have his trust and I knew that I would do anything for him. He once told me that he had wanted a son. He had an only daughter, my cousin Betty and he regarded me as his own son.

Each summer we took long hikes into the hills and walked for miles on country roads. I couldn't keep up with his long strides, so I ended up running most of the way. Eventually I became extremely fit. He always inspired me and gave me hope when I felt low and directions when I felt lost. I knew that I could rely on him for anything.

One day, at the end of the summer vacation he said, "So, tell your mother that next year we'll be expecting you for the usual summer vacation. But we'll be staying in Bourgoin where we've got things to do."

"Yeah," I said enthusiastically.

I had heard that the area was rumored to be a stronghold for Resistance activity against the Germans. But it was no surprise that no one ever spoke about it openly. I couldn't help but wonder why Uncle David had chosen to move to this particular region. Since he told me about his connection with the Resistance, I wondered about his role in the organization. Was he involved in undercover activities like Papa had been? I didn't know for sure, but I thought 'Some day, I'll find out.'

* * *

In the summer of 1943 I was invited again to join Betty and my uncle and aunt in Bourgoin. I was elated that I could enjoy Betty's company again. It was my second trip to the area, and I had nothing but fond memories of pastoral scenes, lingering sunsets, fun walks and rolling in the grass with Betty.

That June afternoon things were different. Uncle David came to meet me at the train station, and we drove straight to a farm.

"George, you'll be staying at a nice farm, this summer," he said.

"But I don't understand. Aren't we going to the house where you live?"

As we were approached the farm he explained. "Ethel and Betty escaped from a raid in Grenoble. Ethel is hiding on another farm. Betty found refuge in a convent nearby. You'll be staying on this farm."

"What about you, Uncle?"

"I'll be in and out. I'll see that you're all taken care of. By the way, you will be given a job at the farm."

I winced at the news. This wasn't going to be the usual fun like previous summers. David seemed in a hurry. He introduced me to the farmer, "Mr. Didier, this is my nephew. He'll be of great help to you. He is a fine young man."

He turned to me and said, "Mr. Didier will take over now. George, I'll see you in a few days."

* * *

Before I tell about my involvement with the Resistance, I need to recount how the movement began in that particular region of France, and how Uncle David took part in this historic chapter of resistance fighting. Bourgoin was in the county of Bas-Dauphine. Jean Moulin had carved areas of the Resistance into regions.

Each region was designated by a number: Region 1, 2, 3 and so forth.

Region 1, our region, covered the county of Bas-Dauphine. The three chiefs who shared the responsibility for the area were Cordier, Raoul and Remy.

Bourgoin and Jallieu, two little towns in the Bas-Dauphine, eventually became the fiercest centers of the Resistance in that part of France. Although most people in the town knew about the subversive activities, secrecy was bravely maintained by the majority of the citizens.

Maurice Rulliere, a local leader in the Resistance, chronicled the events that transpired from the Spring of 1941 to Liberation Day, the

23rd of August, 1944, in a little book published in French.2 These are the highlights of these historic events:

On February 11, 1941, a small group of men set out to organize the Resistance in that region. They formed three sections to cover the area between the two towns. Each section was given a code name.

They met secretly in a local bar, the cafe des Marroniers in Jallieu.

Captain Remy was appointed in charge of the first section called by the code name "Combat." In his group were Jean Duclos, Ruy nicknamed "Albert", Leon Profique and Maurice Berger ("Lili"). Other names were added later on. Among them were Marcel Bonnet-Gonnet nicknamed "Robert", his brother Emile "Marius", Gaby Vassel known as "Johnny", Pierre Falcoz known as "Pierrot", and Marcel Joannin known as "Valmy." Remy's wife completed the group.

The second section, with code name "Liberation", became the responsibility of Claude Chary, whose nickname was "Cordier." This was the section that Uncle David belonged to which eventually would become my section also.

---

[2] It was published in 1982 by Bellier Press, Lyon, under the title "Resistance En Bas-Dauphine: Histoire du Secteur VII, Liberateur de Bourgoin et de Jallieu."

Henri Collet was appointed captain of the third section named "Franc-Tireur."

All three sections were to keep in constant communication through the use of young teenagers recruited to be messengers.

Georges Ivanoff, a physician, close friend and colleague of my uncle, chose the code name "Raoul". In 1942, Henri Collet, Chief of the third section "Franc-Tireur", became too ill to continue and Ivanoff (Raoul) was asked to succeed him.

Although these small groups of guerrilla fighters were functioning independently, they agreed to share secret Germans troop movements in the area.

Each section was broken down in teams of six men, called "sizaines." and were assigned to specific tasks.

One section was assigned to strategic planning. Another to printing messages and newsletters. Another to delivering messages using runners. Finally, some were responsible for collecting arms, explosives, and helping with air drops from Allied airplanes.

One morning "Cordier", the Chief in charge of our section received a phone call that he had been fingered by someone as a subversive. Before he had a chance to leave his house to go into hiding in the mountains, he was arrested. He had been designated to be the future leader of the new organization, known as the "M.U.R.", which stood for the Mouvements Unis de la Resistance, a national movement.

A few days later, Cordier was released for lack of evidence and shortly thereafter took charge of the "M.U.R." Unfortunately, his two companions, the brothers Vallet and Chevrier were not released and were never heard from after that.

Acts of valor and bravery were common. One day in 1941, two young boys in their teens, Georges Ducros, also known as "Bob" and Gino Barbisan, came out of the movie theater "Le Femina" and calmly approached the building of the Legion of Honor on the Rue de la Republique where Germans were stationed. They planted a bomb near the building and it exploded minutes later as they fled unharmed. Many of these teenagers became unsung heroes in the war.

By November, 1942, the Germans had moved about 150 soldiers to the Bourgoin area where they occupied silos, the train station, barns, government buildings, local schools, and hotels.

In December, 1942, Jo Raffin and Robert Barruel sneaked into the gendarmerie, stole several rifles and destroyed the transmitter used to send messages about local troop movements. This was a dangerous but a fantastic coup to pull off.

The next morning, Raffin and Barruel and their buddies met at the Cafe des Marroniers. Uncle David had invited me to attend the meeting, and I felt exhilirated to be included in such esteemed company.

Cordier called the meeting to order and started with a question. "Who's gonna do the next one?"

"What does Remy say? He's the one who gives the final orders," said Maurice, a veteran fighter.

"Well, he says we should blast the high tension wires on the metal pillars near the station, then blow up the railroad before the Krauts get any more reinforcements," said Cordier.

"Yeah, but when are we going to get the plastic from the air drops?" asked George Touquet, a saboteur with a great deal of experience.

"They'll be coming any time now. We just need to get our team in place and be ready to move as soon as the plastic gets here," said Marius who had just come back from Lyon with a stash of explosives and arms.

"Remy said we should ask the team of Martin and Paul Falcoz," said Maurice.

"Fine, let's get the word out to them. David, would you mind sending George on this mission?" said Cordier.

I could feel my heart pounding and my ears burning.

David answered without hesitation. "George will be ready. Won't you George?"

"Yes, I will," I said in my most grown-up voice.

"Good idea. Let's get it done," ordered Cordier.

Later that day, uncle David, added a few words of caution. "George, this is a very delicate and dangerous mission. We count on you to pull it off. It's scheduled for tomorrow."

"I am ready, Uncle. Just tell me what to do."

I felt a mixture of anxiety and excitement. Danger? I had had enough of that already. But this new assignment sounded like something important. Perhaps lives were at stake. This had remained secret. I thought that the assumption was that if I didn't know the potential danger, I wouldn't get panicky and fail to perform.

I felt something big was being entrusted to me. There was no room for failure. I had to deliver or else they would never trust me again.

I would never be told about the consequences of my actions.

*   *   *

The next day, just before sunrise David, awakened me. The sky was bluish gray, heavily shrouded in clouds. The sun was showing through the clouds and the air outside smelled fresh like a cool mint.

"Hurry up, George. We've got work to do," David said.

I nodded and said, "I'll be right there. Just give me five."

He must have been up for hours. He was alert, dressed, shaven, and busy with papers all laid out on the floor.

"I am preparing a load for you, George. Will you be ready?"

"I'm ready. Just tell me what you want me to do?"

"You'll deliver a set of envelopes to a man in Jallieu," he said, "and you'll stash those envelopes under your shirt."

"What's the man's name?" I asked.

"Mr. Falcoz. His code name is "Pierrot." Remember we talked about him at the meeting yesterday," he said.

"How do I get there?"

"You'll take Mr. Didier's bike. You'll go down the winding road and past Jallieu and you'll turn right. Off the main road, you'll see an isolated path. There'll be a fence along side. Follow that path for about 5 kilometers. You'll see Falcoz dressed in overalls. Stop. Give the password. "Les Enfants du Paradis" (The Children of Paradise). He'll come to you and take the package of documents. Got that."

"Got it."

"What if I get stopped?" I asked.

"Just say that you're going to visit your grandmother, who is ill, and that you got lost along the way," David explained.

"What if they ask for papers?"

"You don't have any. You'll go under an assumed name. Your name will be George Muratti. It's an Italian name," he said.

"Why an Italian name?" I inquired.

"There are reasons. I don't have time to explain it now. Just do it," he said.

It really didn't matter to me. I thought he had good reasons, and that was good enough for me. All I cared about was getting into the action. After my last name change, I was getting used to the idea of new names.

"One more thing," he added.

"What is it?"

"You musn't tell your mother. I'll tell her that you're enjoying this vacation and that you want to stay a little longer in the countryside. I know that she won't object if that's what you want," he said.

"That's fine with me," I said with some excitement in my voice.

Finally I would have an active part in this bloody war besides running away all the time. Being a participant would help my fears and my feelings of helplessness and frustration. Of course I had no idea of the danger involved.

* * *

Minutes later, I was coasting down the road on an old farm bike and I was pedaling faster and faster. I could feel my heart thumping inside my chest.

My first mission. I've got to do well or they'll never trust me to do another one. But what if I get caught?

I had heard that Jorge Semprun, a boy from around Bourgoin, had been caught and never returned to his home. No one knew where he was sent. Years later, I learned that he had been sent to Buchenwald and that he had miraculously survived

I realized the enormity of the risk I was taking in this mission. Should I have accepted to join the Resistance? Wasn't I too young? No one would have expected me to accept. Would Uncle David have been disappointed? Angry?

I had just passed Jallieu. I was about to make a right turn to take the lonely road ahead and I was blinded by the sun for a moment. I heard a voice shouting behind me, "Halt. Halt. Papiere!"

I got off my bike and turned around. A German soldier with shiny boots and thick glasses stood waiting for an answer.

"Halt. Halt. Papiere," he repeated.

"Je n'ai pas des papiers. Je vais voir ma grand-mere qui est malade," I said (I don't have any papers. I'm going to see my grandmother, who is ill).

He looked at me with scornful eyes, as if wondering what to say next. He didn't speak French, and he stood there in front of me, obviously wondering what I had said. An awkward silence filled the space between us. Our eyes fixed on each other, reflecting unspoken feelings of dread and suspicion.

Without further explanation, he lowered his rifle, and waved me on. Did he see something in my eyes that reminded him of himself? Or of one of his sons? I'll never know. But I thought that silence sometimes can communicate feelings more than words can ever do.

I held my breath, got on my bike, let out a big sigh, and started pedaling furiously.

I arrived at the assigned destination by mid-day. The man I was supposed to meet, Monsieur Falcoz saw me coming and he stood there and remained silent, as if waiting for me to say something. I got off my bike and said the password "Les Enfants du Paradis." He smiled and asked, "Ca va? Tu as l'enveloppe?" (Things O.K.?. Do you have the envelope?)

"Oui, sous ma chemise." (Yes, under my shirt). I unbuttoned my shirt and handed him the flat envelope.

Falcoz thanked me, turned around and waved me goodbye. "Bonjour a ton oncle."

Without looking back, I jumped on my bike and raced back to the farm. Mr. Didier had given me a day off, so I could fulfill my duty.

I felt proud and brave like a soldier who had just accomplished a heroic mission.

* * *

Months later, I learned that being caught in the act of transporting secret documents for the Resistance meant sure death by execution or arrest and deportation to a concentration camp. I heard that a boy named Helie de Saint Marc, had been arrested while crossing the Demarcation Line from the Occupied to the Unoccupied Zone.

Years later, I read in his memoir that he had been sent to Compiegne, a holding camp, before being deported to Buchenwald, where he almost died of starvation and exhaustion while waiting for the Americans to reach the camp.

Running away over the past two years had not diminished the risk of dying, I reasoned. Fighting might be better than running scared.

*   *   *

The next day David said to me, "Good work, George. I'm very proud of you. Mr. Cordier heard about your mission and he personally wants to thank you."

"Really? He wants to see me?" I said.

"Yes. Just meet him in the lobby of the Hotel Chenavas. He'll be looking for you. His wife Odette will be there too."

"That's great. I'll be there," I said.

Odette, had come to ask Raoul permission to join her husband, Cordier, in the hills.

I arrived in the lobby of the hotel half an hour early and was surprised to see several SS officers in full uniform, chatting and apparently waiting. I had no idea why they were there, but I had learned to trust my instincts and sensed that trouble was brewing. Was it a trap? Had someone squealed on Cordier's arrival?

I introduced myself to Odette. I whispered to her, "My name is George. David said that Mr. Cordier asked to meet him here."

She was a charming and pretty woman with long blond hair, hazel eyes, a slim figure, wearing a light summer dress and walking shoes.

She seemed pleased to meet me but she appeared uneasy as she noted the German officers pacing back and forth.

She whispered into my ear, "My husband will be arriving shortly. Please, wait there in the corner of the lobby to see what transpires before you come to meet him. This could mean trouble."

The officers kept conversing in German, looking at their watches, waiting for someone to arrive.

At two o'clock, Cordier entered the lobby. He was an impressive figure. Over six feet tall, a barrel chest, arms the size of a tree trunk, a bushy hairstyle, a thick mustache, corduroy trousers and heavy hiking boots.

The commanding SS officer, who was wearing a monocle, came forward and asked with a thick German accent, "Are you Mister Cordier?"

"Yes, I am," Cordier said.

"And is this your wife?" the officer asked.

"Yes."

"Do you know why she is here?" the officer continued.

"She came to meet me after my return from a visit to relatives in Lyon."

"Ach, so. I see. And who exactly did you visit in Lyon, may I ask?"

"My cousin, my uncle and my aunt" Cordier said, slightly annoyed.

"Ach, so. I see. It just so happens that my assistant checked out that you did not come from the Bahnhof (train depot)."

"Well, maybe your assistant didn't check well enough," Cordier replied.

"Do not be impertinent with an SS officer! This may cost you your life!" the officer bellowed.

Cordier may have overstepped his boundaries. He should have been more careful. It was always risky to answer a question sarcastically, and indeed, it could end up badly. It would take only one bad answer to irritate the questioner and lead to a charge of resisting and insulting an SS officer, an accusation often followed by a summary execution.

Cordier's face relaxed, and he immediately retracted. "Well, I did take a detour and I must have been seen on the other side of Jallieu, on my way here. That's what I meant."

"I see. Mister Cordier, you are a very smart man."

They both threw cold glares at each other. The officer was becoming impatient and fidgeting while bending a leather whip in his hand. There was an awkward pause. He must have felt like his prey was slipping through his fingers.

"And were are you going now with your wife?" the officer asked.

"I guess, we'll be going home, if that's all right with you, Herr colonel?" said Cordier.

"I believe that you're not telling the truth. I have information that your wife came here to ask you if she could leave with you to the hills?"

"I don't know how anyone could have given you this information. She just called me a few hours ago," Cordier said with a firm tone. "If so, I'd like to meet this person who seems to know."

"We respect our sources and never betray them," the officer said in his harsh Germanic accent.

"Well, I'm at your disposal," Cordier said.

"You will stay in this town until we'll conclude our investigation and we will inform you of our decision in due time. Good-bye," the officer said.

The officer clacked his heels, extended his arm and exclaimed "Heil Hitler!" as did his assistants in unison. They turned around and marched out of the lobby. Odette was completely frozen.

"Quelle veine!"(what luck) said Cordier to his wife and friends.

Odette seemed to regain her composure.

"I have a hunch who might have squealed," she said.

"We must find out. The sooner the better," said her husband.

"I think it's Mrs. Charmaine, the concierge next door. She's always watching through her window who goes in and out. The old bitch!" Odette said.

"Let's go and talk to her," said one of Cordier's friends.

Odette broke in the conversation. "But first, let me introduce you to David's nephew. He came especially to meet my husband and all of you," Odette said.

I came forward.

Cordier extended his hand.

"I've heard about your mission. You've done a fine job and we're all very proud of you. Also lucky to have you on our side. Your uncle

David is a great guy. He is a key man for us. We all love him. Tell him how much we appreciate him and his team."

We shook hands. As they were preparing to leave, Odette turned to me.

"George, do you want to come along with us and see how we handle this problem?"

"I'd love to," I said.

We all climbed into Cordier's truck, which Odette had driven to the hotel, and we drove to Mrs. Charmaine's house.

We found her at home, knitting, in her old rocking chair. She was an elderly widow, a loner with a suspicious mind who was not liked in the neighborhood.

Cordier knocked on the door.

"Mrs. Charmaine, please open. It's Odette and her husband."

Hunched over and wearing an old garish robe she opened the door.

"What do you want from me," she said.

"We just want to ask you a few questions," said Cordier.

"Everybody comes here and wants to ask me a few questions," the old woman said.

"And who else came here to ask you?" Cordier asked.

"I don't have to tell you. It's none of your business," said the old woman.

"You don't need to tell us. We know that you spoke to the German officers," Cordier said.

"So? It's none of your business," the woman replied.

"I believe it is, Mrs. Charmaine. And I'm telling you that if you give them any more information about us out there, fighting for France, you will not live long after that. Understood?" Cordier said with a determined tone in his voice.

She remained quiet. Frozen and shaken.

Cordier repeated his admonition. "Understood?" while he glared icily at her.

She nodded, unable to say another word. I wondered if she could be trusted, even on the promise of a threat? It was doubtful.

But it didn't matter, because Cordier and Odette were leaving that night for the maquis camps, deep into the impenetrable forest of the hills.

* * *

Later, in July 1944, Cordier (his real name was Claude Chary) was promoted to be the head of the F.F.I. (French Forces of the Interior) in that region for all military and civilian affairs by General Koenig of the overseas French Forces. It was truly one of the highest honors a local chief of the Resistance could get and Uncle David said to me how proud he was for having served under his command.

23- The Farm

As I bicycled back to the farm, I was reliving the confrontation between Cordier and the SS officer. It had been a close call, and I wondered whether the colonel had another plan to catch Cordier. Would he go back to Mrs. Charmaine and get more information? Would she squeal again or keep quiet, given the harsh warning from Cordier?

Cordier was a true leader, fearless, smart and powerful, and I imagined that he would not get caught again by the colonel.

I was so proud to have pulled off my mission and felt so good about being congratulated by Cordier and his wife, Odette, that I couldn't wait to tell Uncle David and see his reaction.

I felt like a hero. I was in the Resistance and I was helping in the war effort. It was the right thing for me to do and now I could be trusted with other assignments. But I would have to wait until I met David again.

It was back to the usual farm routine and my apprenticeship of becoming a good shepherd.

On a warm July day, the alarm woke me at 5 A.M. I jumped out of bed, had a bowl of cafe au lait and downed a couple of buttered toasts. The price I had to pay for living in hiding on the farm was to take twenty cows to pasture every day about six kilometers from the farm.

Mr. Didier gave me a long wooden rod to steer the squadron of cows and said, "You take along Sunshine, our dog. He knows what to do. He'll be a big help. You just let him lead the cows and bring them back. All you have to do is call him and tell him you're ready to come back. Simple, isn't it?"

I nodded, trying not to show my unease. The closest I came to know cows was to watch the 'laughing cow' on the little cheese packages sold in the grocery stores and the ones I had seen from the train window, peacefully grazing in the pastures.

But with Mr. Didier's encouragement and faith in his dog Sunshine, I felt reasonably sure that I could cope with the task.

Sunshine was a beautiful golden German shepherd, and although he seemed to just tolerate me, he was always nice to me in front of Mr. Didier.

"Sit, ole boy! Be nice to George!" Didier would say to Sunshine.

Sunshine would sit, then lie down and roll over in front of me, as if saying 'You see, I know what my master wants me to do.' As soon as Mr. Didier would turn his back, Sunshine would show me his teeth as if saying 'I don't really care for you.' I hoped he would take pity on me, and I put my whole destiny into his paws.

That morning as we began meandering down the road I took the lead in front of the twenty cows and left it up to Sunshine to bring in the rear. To give myself a sense of meaning for this utterly demoralizing task, I imagined that I was on another mission of sorts: That of leading these poor devils to safety, while the war was raging on. The cows walked sluggishly, swinging their belly from side to side, ringing the bells hanging around their neck.

Three cows had wandered off the road towards a ditch. I turned around, whistled and yelled "Sunshine, get them, get them quick!" I whistled till my lungs hurt.

I couln't see Sunshine anywhere. Where the hell was he? He wasn't in the rear. I looked ahead, and in the distance I saw Sunshine running off, all by himself. Desperate, I screamed as loud as I could.

"Sunshine, come back here, you hear! Come back right now, this minute!"

The more I yelled, the farther he ran.

"Damn you. I knew I couldn't trust you."

I was dumfounded. Frantic, I yelled at these bovine creatures at the top of my voice to get the hell back on the road. They all ignored me and wandered off, totally oblivious and uncaring of my feelings and my screaming. As soon as I rallied two or three of them, two more wandered off in the opposite direction, as if to say, 'We have a life of our own, you know. This is not our problem.' My only help was my rod, which I used deliberately to remind them who was boss, since my canine assistant had decided to go AWOL!

After an hour of these heroic maneuvers, the cows and I finally reached the fenced-in pasture down the road, just in time before I collapsed, totally exhausted, yet thankful that the first half of the assignment was over. I thought that I would rather carry on another mission for the Resistance, because I had more of a feel for handling tight situations with the enemy than second guessing what these damn beasts were doing to me.

Sitting in the shade of a huge oak tree, I watched these poor devils slowly chewing their cud, while my mind kept ruminating: 'I'm not cut out to be a cow retriever. We don't have cowboys in France. I'll never succeed at this sort of thing. Will I be able to last out the summer without being kicked out by Mr. Didier? And that damn Sunshine. How will I explain his disappearance? Didier will be angry with me if I lose a few cows, but if I lose Sunshine, that will be the guillotine, for sure!

And as the day slipped by, my eyes felt heavy, and I decided to nod off for a while, resting my head on my lunch box.

A truck, letting out huge blasts and puffs of black smoke on the road below the pasture, woke me up. The cows were all over the meadow, some lying in the sun, others grazing and chewing happily to their hearts content.

Again, I yelled "Sunshine, you son of a bitch. Where are you? I softened my tone of voice and said, "Come here, Sunshine. Come here, big boy."

No answer. I whistled. Nothing. Not a sign of Sunshine. What was I to do? The sun was just setting down over the horizon. I had overslept, and there was no time to waste. I needed Sunshine desperately, but he didn't seem to care. That damn dog! How could he do this to me? A human being! I wasn't just another dog!

Brandishing my gnarly rod, I began my task of rallying the bovine troops. I felt like the Sergeant in charge of a bunch of drunken renegades from the Foreign Legion who couldn't care less about my orders, let alone my feelings.

After an hour of jogging back and forth between the front and the rear of the herd, while stroking their backs and rears, I finally got them to follow a lead cow, seemingly the wisest of the lot. We marched back up the road all the way to the farm. About two hundred yards before reaching the barn, I saw Sunshine, happily wagging his tail and joining the crowd.

Mr. Didier was standing at the entrance of the barn.

"Isn't he a wonderful dog, this Sunshine? Bet you, he made your day pretty easy, didn't he?"

I threw a dirty look at Sunshine, "Oh! yes, Monsieur Didier. I don't know what I would have done without him!"

24- Lili and David

Mr. Didier had a short wave radio and each evening we listened to the BBC, getting the latest communiques on the war. Before going down to the cellar, we turned off all the lights, thus pretending to outsiders that all the farmers had gone to bed.

We huddled near the radio, keeping the volume down, trying to catch every word between the statics. "This is the BBC. And now, the latest bulletin on the war on this day of February 13, 1943. The German war machine is running into difficulty. The Russian army continues to inflict more German casualties, and the enemy is struggling to provide more reinforcements. We believe that the German government is trying to recruit more young men from occupied countries to fill the vacancies in the arms factories."

Besides the radio, we had underground newspapers that would publish news, opinions, information, statistics, and latest developments in the Resistance, the German troops, and the war in Europe.

In France we learned that there was a shortage of slave workers, mostly Jews, communists, resistance fighters, in the factories throughout Germany.

To cope with this tremendous shortage, the High German Command ordered the Vichy government to issue an order compelling all Frenchmen, in the draft class of 1939 to 1942 (ages 18-22), to register for the S.T.O. known as Service du Travail Obligatoire (Obligatory Work Service).

It was estimated that approximately fifty percent of those eligible had decided to head for the hills. On the one hand, it was fortunate for the "maquis forces" to get this influx of reinforcement. On the other hand, the question was: How were they to manage these hordes of rebels? They needed fake identity cards, shelter, food supplies, training, discipline, arms, and leadership. How could the maquis forces get all of this in a short period of time? How were the Resistance leaders to make contact with these young men without alerting the Vichy authorities and the Gestapo?

The challenge was overwhelming. The leaders of the maquis had decided that it was best to limit the number of these young men and those who would be admitted into the Resistance would be directed to local farms where they would be oriented and trained.

Others had an alternative. They could volunteer to join special State services such as state police, gendarmerie, railroad duty or silo work. Indirectly, they could help the Resistance by their "unintentional" neglect and failure to perform for the Germans or the Vichy government.

The rest could remain in the community and work for the German army but specialize in "errors of commission." For example, Jacques Stoklin and Maurice Barnez, two such young men, succeeded in putting excessive amounts of toxic chemicals in the barrels of sauerkraut destined to feed the German troops. By the time the SS investigation was over Jacques and Maurice had disappeared into the night fog enveloping the hillside.

* * *

On a cold and foggy night of November 1943, a new platoon of Feldgendarmes arrived at the Hotel Chenavas. The Germans were redoubling their efforts to capture dissidents. Security was getting tighter and Resistance assignments were becoming more difficult.

In Bourgoin and Jallieu, the morale of the Resistance guerrilla fighters had remained high. The maquis forces were eagerly waiting for arms supplies from the Allies, but none had been delivered for several weeks.

Captain "Remy" had been in communication with the British Command for Parachute Drops and Landings to establish the sites, the number of containers, the contents and the exact dates and times for the delivery. It was up to Captain "Raoul" to coordinate the team that was going to receive the material, store it, distribute it, and finally get rid of the parachutes and the containers.

There were problems. Remy and Raoul needed to choose the right weather, anticipate the D.C.A. (Defense Contre Avions—the anti-aircraft fire)—and the intervention by the Luftwaffe. Not an easy task but a tremendous responsibility.

Parachute drops would typically occur during the full moon, between ten o'clock and midnight. Advance notice would come through the BBC coded messages.

On March 10, 1944, the message came through" Le robinet fuit." (The faucet is leaking. The faucet is leaking. Repeat. The faucet is leaking.) The message was repeated three times. The team was ready at the site of the village of Paleysin at exactly ten o'clock. But ten o'clock came and went. No plane in sight. Had the plane been shot down? Was it a false alarm? Was it a trap set up by the Germans? Or was it simply that the mission had been aborted? Finally, the team had gone home, waiting for further instructions.

On Wednesday, March 22, a new message came through. "Visitez le Louvre. Repeat: Visitez le Louvre (Visit the Louvre)." Everything went precisely on time. Huge numbers of containers carried by enormous parachutes, filled with machine guns, rifles, grenades, explosives and pistols, landed at the site of the village of Paleysin.

The wind from the north was fierce, and a German alert had been given as soon as the British plane had been sighted over Bourgoin. By the time the German stukas filled the air, the British pilot had vanished. The mission had been a success.

By April and May, more parachute drops had taken place in the "Bois de Roche" near Artas and another one near Hyacinthe Fouilleux.

By August, there was enough weaponry to arm all sections in the region. Huge caches of arms were stored in silos, in barns, in chicken coops, and even in the building for emergency supplies next to the Feldgendarmerie.

Now everyone in the local Resistance was ready. Plans for demolishing the power lines and the electric transformers for the local factories vital to the war effort were made.

From July to August 1944, the guerrilla fighters went on full time schedules. Trains collided and derailed. Depots went up in flame. Silos full of food supplies for the Germans exploded. Official French guards of the railroads called in sick on the days targeted for the interventions.

Attacks were made almost daily. The pace was frantic. When arrests were made, these setbacks slowed the action in some areas.

French collaborators were helping the Gestapo throughout the area. On a tip by an informer, the Gestapo arrested Marcel Petit while he was on his way home. The following week, he was deported. The next day, the brothers Garrivier were caught in their own garage with a huge stash of arms and explosives. They were arrested and shot on the spot. Maxence Tavel, a young teacher, was apprehended in his classroom. He too disappeared among the hordes of deportees.

Raids by the Germans became a weekly occurrence. Everyone in Bourgoin and Jallieu could be a suspect. Despite fear and terror sweeping in the whole region, guerrilla attacks continued relentlessly.

But by the summer of 1944, things were looking brighter and more promising. Allied troops were on French soil and making huge inroads into the German lines.

*　*　*

I remained in my little farm, hiding and remaining quiet as a mouse. Every day, I heard about more arrests. Mr. Didier would let me listen to the BBC and the local station announcing more arrests and reprisals.

I had not heard from Uncle David for some time, and I began to worry about him. Had he been caught? Why wasn't he calling? Was he just being cautious? We knew that many of the lines had been tapped.

After two weeks of silence, a call came in.

"It's for you, George. It's your uncle," yelled Mr. Didier.

I rushed to the phone in the hallway.

"Uncle, I am so glad it's you. I was worried."

"I'm fine. I was away on a trip. Couldn't call you then. Will see you in a few days. Got stuff to tell you. Be prepared. Au revoir."

I was relieved. He sounded in a hurry. Didn't even let me get a word in before he hung up. Again, I was left with my own speculations. Why did he say a few days? Why not today? What stuff was he going to tell me? Now, I was trying to fill in the blanks and my mind was full, with both my inner voices fighting each other.

On June 6, we listened to a new coded message, "Le premier accroc coute deux cents francs" (the first rip costs two hundred francs.) We knew then that the Allies had landed on the coast of

Normandy. It was called "Operation Overlord." This was truly a historic day!

*   *   *

A flurry of messages kept coming, urging the population to a general uprising. But the fears for a massive bloody reprisal was so great that Captain Raoul countermanded the order. He said that we needed to wait for the German debacle. Also, we had to reduce the number of arrests taking place on a daily basis. He feared for his own men. Several had been captured the previous weeks.

Uncle David didn't call in a few days as he had promised. I worried that something terrible had happened. I had heard Mr. Didier whisper to someone that the Gestapo had captured a key member. Was it Uncle David?

I learned that the Gestapo had broken into "Lili" Berger's home. Lili had been a key leader in the local resistance movement and a close friend of Uncle David. They both worked as a team. Uncle David had the greatest admiration and respect for Lili Berger.

A month later, I heard the whole story from a guerrilla fighter, Jacques, who had escaped the ordeal and had witnessed the gory tragedy.

The Gestapo had found a short wave transmitter in the fields which they had traced to "Lili." They had yanked him out of bed and had started torturing him in front of his wife, twisting his arms and neck, putting needles under his nails and in his mouth, while bombarding him with questions. "Where did you get this English transmitter? Who is Pierre Bonnas? Where is David Distel, the dentist? You will speak or you will die." Berger never gave in, Jacques said. He never gave any valid answer.

They took Lili to the Feldgendarmerie in Bourgoin. Torture sessions continued but he refused to talk. When the pain became excruciating, he passed out. They showed him photographs of him shaking hands with Pierre Bonnas, a known Resistance fighter and with Uncle David. But "Lili" then made up a story which they did not believe. He said that he had just stumbled on the transmitter while walking in the fields on his way home. It didn't matter. They didn't believe him anyway. The Feldgendarmes continued the interrogation.

"We have Pierre Bonnas. He told us all about you. Why not confess and make it easier on yourself!"

Lili guessed that this was just a ruse and refused to change his story. He did carry some revealing document in his trousers, but in their excitement, the Germans had not frisked him. He suddenly had requested an urgent call for the bathroom to relieve himself, and while in the bathroom, he quickly flushed the critical paper down the toilet.

Unable to get anything out of him, the Feldgendarme transferred him to the Gestapo headquarters where Klaus Barbie, the Chief of the Gestapo in Lyon, held court. They withheld food and water for eight days, but Lili still refused to give in.

By then, he looked like a walking dead. The jailers called in Raymond, nicknamed "Ugly Mug", who was an expert in exquisite and sophisticated torture. But after several hours of vicious beating and torturing, he too, gave up when nothing would bend Lili's will and determination.

They sent Lili to the Montluc prison and threw him naked into a cell. Several well known prisoners (among them, General Chevallier,

Monsignor Vodenic, industrialist Dechelette) had offered to give up their water ration, so Lili could wash his bloody and dirty wounds.

The following week, Lili and his new companions were thrown into train cattle cars, which rolled non-stop for seven days. They were given one tuna can and one roll per man and nothing to drink. Seventy five men, all exhausted and reeking with all the odors of human excretion were lying helpless on a bed of straw.

Suddenly the train stopped. Jacques succeeded in prying one of the sliding doors so that it slid ajar. Lili made a dash for the opening but the butt of a rifle hit him and broke his shoulder. The last hope for an escape had gone for good.

The reprisal for such an act meant that five men had to be executed. They were shot the next day. The train then continued on its deathly destination. It stopped briefly at Reims.

In the station Lili managed to scribble a few words onto a piece of paper that he rolled with saliva into a papier mache and threw through the thin opening. A rail worker caught it and delivered it to Lili's family. It said briefly, 'Nothing told. Hope is eternal.'

The locomotive blew its whistle and the train started its slow, tikatikat, tikatikat sound on the long smooth rails across the gray landscape.

Next was the final stop at the camp at Neuengamme. The newcomers were marched out into the smelly yards full of mud and stagnant puddles. Lili and his friends dove to the ground, desperately slurping the muddy waters. Their first night was spent in a cellar infested with rats. Their only remaining question was "When will death come to deliver them from the enemy." Finally, the black silence enveloped the poor souls to their last destination. Miraculously, Jacques was the only one to survive the ordeal and to recount the story in its hideous details.

*   *   *

I had just returned from my tribulations with the cows and Sunshine and Mr. Didier called me into the living room. I sensed that something was wrong. I feared that he had been tipped off by another farmer about my less than lustrous performance. I was anticipating the ax to fall.

He looked worried and somber. I was sure that he was going to fire me and call for my uncle to get me.

"I've got some bad news," he said with a sad tone of voice.

"What is it, Monsieur Didier?"

"I've just been told that your uncle has been arrested this morning. Right now, as we speak, he is at the gendarmerie. He was apprehended by the brigadier of the gendarmerie, Mr. LeMaire who just called me himself."

I was dumfounded. Something had to be done and we just couldn't sit here and do nothing. How could this have happened? Someone must have squealed. But who? Was it Mrs. Charmaine? "What can we do? Should we go and talk to the brigadier?" I cried out.

"That would be too dangerous. And you'd be arrested."

"Is there anyone we can call about this?"

"I'll call Raoul, the Captain of the local Resistance. He knows everyone in Bourgoin and Jallieu. You know that he is a doctor, and most of the people, including the gendarmes, were his patients at one time or another. He can talk to LeMaire."

He got Raoul on the phone.

"David has been caught. They've got him at the gendarmerie. They'll deport him. He is Jewish, you know. He surely will die unless we do something."

"I'm on my way. I know the brigadier and I'll make the bastard listen to me. I'll call you later."

Hours passed. I paced back and forth while watching through the windows for Raoul's car. What was holding him up? Did he himself get into trouble?

Mr. Didier kept giving me hope. I wanted to call Ethel, my aunt, but Mr. Didier didn't think it was a good idea in case the lines were bugged. The wait was getting to be intolerable. Finally, Raoul appeared in the driveway.

"Cm'on in," Didier shouted at Raoul before he knocked on the door.

"It's been a long day. I've got lots to say," Raoul said.

We all sat down at the table in the dining room.

"Bring us some hot cider," Didier said to his wife, who was busy in the kitchen.

"Well?" Didier asked impatiently.

Raoul unbuttoned his heavy furry parka, sat down and gave his report. "Let me start by saying that David is free and he is fine but shaken."

"Well, will you tell us how you did it?" asked Didier.

David was safe, and that was all I needed to know. I kept quiet and listened.

"I got there, and they had been questioning him for hours about his involvement with the maquis. He kept denying the allegations. Someone had squealed and had reported him as a Jew and as a traitor. He was being charged with subversive activities, treason to France, abetting the underground and conspiring against the German war effort."

"Did he give in?"

"No. He kept denying everything."

"How do you know?"

"I spoke to Brigadier LeMaire. He is the one who arrested David.

LeMaire is a patient of mine. I know his medical and family history. He's been cheating on his wife for years and he has lied even to his priest."

"What a stroke of luck!" Didier said..

Raoul went on. "So, I said to LeMaire, I know that you know that the life of this man, David, is in your hands. You can send him to his death or you can release him and set him free right now before this matter goes to the Gestapo."

Mrs. Didier brought in the hot cider.

"That's good cider, my friends. Let me tell you what followed. LeMaire wouldn't give in. He cited his duty as a good and moral citizen and law enforcer. I pointed out to him that I knew otherwise. In fact I reminded him of the gonorrheal infection for which I treated him on several occasions and all that this could imply to the community and to his wife. He looked at me in stony silence."

"And then he gave in?"

"No. Not that easy. He started threatening me too, implying that he could hold me as an accessory, and that I, too, could get the same punishment."

"Some nerve, the bastard. I bet he probably works closely with the Gestapo," said Didier.

"Yeah, I think he does. Then I pulled my last weapon, and I said to him, LeMaire, I don't think you realize that my men know that I am here. If I don't return with David, there will be no gendarmerie left in this town and no brigadier either."

"You pulled no punches," Didier said.

"Well, he backed off. The brigadier glared at me with an icy look and finally gave in. "All right. I'll release him and let you go. But I expect that some day you'll return the favor."

We all looked at each other, partly relieved, partly incredulous. Raoul continued. "David came out of the cell and we departed without saying a word. We had played hard ball and we just got lucky."

"Raoul, that was simply fantastic," said Didier.

"David went back to see Ethel, who knew nothing about the episode."

Raoul said. "You are so lucky to have such a nice uncle, George."

I was so thankful that I could have kissed him, but I held back, feeling that it was not a manly thing to do. So, I simply smiled and said, "Thank you Mr. Raoul for what you did."

* * *

In the summer of 1944, Uncle David became an officer in the F.F.I. (French Forces of the Interior) and later won several medals for bravery and courage while fighting for the liberation of the rest of France. Many years later when he died in New York he was given a special honor guard from a French Overseas delegation at his funeral.

25- Mr. Kleber

At the end of summer I returned to Lyon to resume my classes at the Lycee Ampere.

During the summer I had changed my name to Muratti and I had to remember to go back to my other new name of Bercovici. I had changed my name so many times during the war that I joked about it with David. "I'm changing names as often as my underwear!" My real challenge was to keep those various identities straight in my mind. Only one mistake could be fatal if my assumed name didn't match my parents's name on their identity papers.

Being on the lookout was a way of life. Mother and I always slept lightly, listening for any suspicious noise even after we retired for the night.

Cousin Betty, who had come from her Bourgoin convent for a weekend, Mother and I were having a pleasant evening at home, when we heard the familiar sound of the marching boots of a German patrol thudding on the street pavement. Suddenly, the marching stopped and someone's fist was pounding on the front door.

"Aufmachen, aufmachen. Schnell. Polizei!"

My heart began to pound. Betty's face turned ashen. Mother whispered.

"Quick, get into the attic both of you. Quick, Hurry!"

There was a small trap in the ceiling that opened into the attic, and could be reached through a walk-in closet where several crates had been piled up. We climbed on top of the crates, opened the trap and slid into a small dark space. Downstairs the pounding continued.

Mother had stayed downstairs to meet them. She unlatched the door, and several officers marched in and yelled.

"We are here to search the apartment. We have reason to believe that you are hiding Jews or French resisters," the SS officer said to Mother.

"Herr Officer, we know nothing about this. We have nothing to hide."

From the attic we could hear the grunts and groans of the SS as they began rummaging through the apartment, turning over furniture, emptying drawers, ripping cushions, kicking cupboards, searching for evidence of Jewishness or traces of French resistance. Betty and I were huddled into this tiny space and barely able to breathe.

In her impeccable pure "hoch deutsch", Mother convinced the officers that she knew nothing and that she was on the side of the Reich. She spoke German like a true German, and that seemed to appease them. They said that they had been tipped off by a neighbor that Jews and subversives were in hiding here. They added that they would keep an eye on the apartment and come back to check again from time to time. They marched out, still holding their automatic guns under their arms. Mother waited another half hour before she called us down from the attic, and we all hugged each other, grateful and relieved.

*   *   *

The trafficking of identity papers was a thriving business during those years. One had to be prepared to change names and have cash. There was a thriving black market for almost anything one might desire: passports, visas, identity cards, food, especially eggs, meat, cigarettes, liquor and guns. The price was commensurate with the high risk of getting caught. In many cases, the French Police and the Milice were part of the network so that if one had an inside connection and money, one was relatively safe from being caught and charged.

Collaborators had a built-in immunity and they functioned with greater ease in this murky world of shady deals. Mother knew how to navigate these perilous waters and somehow always found a way out of the most precarious situations. She knew how to make friends on both sides: the black market dealers and those among the French police that could be bribed.

*   *   *

Soon after the school term began, I found my old friends, Jacques Peju, Andre Pays, and Abe Marcus ready to plan new projects. We called ourselves the "four musketeers" in honor of Alexander Dumas.

We resumed our favored past-time, walking up and down the rue de la Republique, the main street in Lyon, where all the local girls loved to parade up and down from City Hall to the famous Place Bellecour, one of the largest squares in France.

One September afternoon, we spotted a group of girls, with tight sweaters and high heels. They walked slowly, swinging their hips, smiling, and giggling, well aware that we were mesmerized by their slender figure and their seductive legs. We turned around as we passed them, gave them an admiring whistle and hoped that they would join us. The girls loved the flirting game and seemed to enjoy the chase more than the prospect of meeting any of us. The game nowadays would be to question whether these girls practiced "safe sex", not whether or not they would go on a date.

Although I trusted my friends, I never told them of my involvement with the Resistance for fear of implicating them if some day they might be interrogated during an investigation. We shared our hatred of the Germans, our distrust of the French Police and our admiration for the Resistance.

We liked most of our teachers for the most part, although we never knew whether any of them were collaborators with the Germans.

I hated my Latin teacher. His name was Mr. Kleber, but I nicknamed him the "Serpent", a name which became known all over the college.

I suspected that he was a collaborator but could never prove it. He had a Germanic approach to teaching: rigid, cruel and sadistic. We had to memorize pages of Latin verse and had to recite them when we least expected to be called.

One day he called on me.

"Bercovici, recite the two passages of Ovid's Metamorphoses which I assigned last week."

I could feel the adrenaline pouring in my body, my neck muscles becoming hard, my cheeks burning, my throat drying up, my knees giving way, and my brain clouding up. The only Latin phrase that came to mind was "ad absurdum". How absurd, that I should be subjected to this indignity, shades of what I had experienced a few years ago, when Mr. Himmler, the teacher at the Strasbourg school, had delighted in humiliating me in front of the whole class.

After a few minutes of excruciating silence in this cold, gray, sterile classroom where everyone was frozen in fear, the Serpent's strident voice pierced the air with a final threat.

"Sit down, Bercovici, I shall see you after class."

His parallel to the German Gestapo was undeniable. I felt that the Serpent was really a French turncoat, hoping to detect young French boys who would become trouble for the Vichy government. We all suspected that Kleber had a perverse mind, and wondered what was awaiting the poor souls he ordered to appear after class.

Kleber waited until all the students had left and we were all alone in this huge classroom. Would he give me additional assignments or dream up some other weird punishment?

His voice became modulated and almost pleasant and accompanied by a crooked smile.

"You know, George," he began, "I really don't dislike you. In fact, I rather think that you're a pleasant fellow."

"I am?" I said, dumbfounded.

"I could be very nice to you, George," he continued while smiling, "if you and I developed an understanding about each other."

"I'm not sure I understand," I said, still feeling puzzled.

"I mean, you and I," he said hesitatingly, "could visit each other now and then and have some private time at my place."

I feigned ignorance. No one had ever spoken this way to me before.

He seemed to gain more confidence and in a daring way put his hand on my shoulder, while whispering in my ear, "You have nothing to fear. Just so you be nice to me." As he said that, he put his hand on my crotch.

I shuddered and felt dizzy, totally beside myself with confusion and rage. I made a dash for the door. He didn't make a move. Like the time I ran away from the French police, I headed for the exit and was out of the building before he had a chance to catch up with me.

I never spoke to my friends or to my parents about this encounter but I began to plan a scheme that would get me far away from this evil man. My going to the authorities with that story would be a waste of time and would get me into even more trouble.

I returned to class but never looked the Serpent straight in the eye. He seemed to avoid me which was fine with me.

I told my friends that my aversion for Latin had grown to be as strong as my aversion for German and I said that we were all wasting our time learning Latin, a dead language that was of no use to anyone in the modern world, and that we should be learning something worthwhile like science, which would have more application for us later in life. A dozen students came around to my point of view.

"Yeah, but what do you suggest we do?" they all asked.

"I'll think of something. And when I do, I'll let you know," I said in the same tone that I had heard Cordier speak to his men.

I found the answer. If only I could convince enough students we could approach the Administration and make our stand: We would boycott the school until they would offer Sciences as an alternative to Latin.

Andre, Jacques and Abe agreed to the strategy. They appointed me as their leader and agreed that I should remain incognito for the time being. They volunteered to campaign for me and get as many students as possible to back up the proposal.

The campaign lasted three months.

"We've got close to thirty students. Twenty from the junior year and at least ten or twelve from the senior year," said Abe, my most trusted lieutenant.

It was the end of April and too late to expect any major changes for that year. Our demands were going to be for the following year. It would take at least that long to recruit a new science teacher.

Jacques, Andre, Abe and I had our last meeting. We'd walk into the Dean's office, and I would do the talking as the spokesman for the thirty students rebelling against the Latin curriculum. We chose not to target the Serpent directly. This would undermine the whole operation. Furthermore, we suspected that the Serpent had his own way of putting pressure on the Administration.

We made an appointment with the Dean, Mr. Solangerie.

The next day, the four musketeers knocked on the huge wooden door of the Dean's Office.

"Come in," said a deep voice that sounded like a voice of wisdom.

We marched in.

"Thank you, Sir. We are here to ask you for a change in the curriculum of the school," I said

"And exactly, what did you have in mind?"

"Sir, we, thirty of us, feel that courses in sciences would be more useful and beneficial than a course in Latin. We feel that the school should offer us a choice. Those of us who are headed for a career in the sciences should be able to choose between Latin or Sciences."

The Dean puffed on his pipe, seemingly amused by our demands. We were prepared for a counter-attack, and I was getting ready for the next argument.

"You realize, boys," he said, "that this is a major request and it will take a great deal of thought."

"Yes, Sir. It's a major development, full of potential and promise for the school."

"Well, I'll have to present this request to the Curriculum Committee," he said, while puffing on his pipe, "and you must realize that there is no guarantee that such a request will be granted."

"Yes, we do, Sir. However, the world is headed towards a world of greater scientific technology, and the school will derive a great deal of credit for being so far-sighted. Sir."

"Yes, boys. I see your point," he said, "and I can't say that I was crazy about Latin myself when I was your age.'

Judging by his remark, I felt that we had a fair chance of winning our case. He was identifying with our cause and getting emotionally involved.

I winked at Andre and Abe.

The Dean concluded. "We'll let you know about our decision after the Committee meets at the end of the month."

"Thank you, Sir."

We made an about face and left the office in Indian file, my three lieutenants following behind me.

* * *

During the next Latin class with the Serpent, I felt as if a tremendous load had been lifted off my shoulders. I could breathe more easily, my muscles were relaxed, and I had an inner sense of mastery that I remember to this day.

Would the Curriculum Committee go along with my request? What would the Serpent do when he'd learn that I was the spokesman for the new proposal? How much influence did he swing on the Committee? Would a defeat of my proposal result in retaliation and reprisals as the Germans had done whenever they ran into saboteurs?

I couldn't sleep, thinking over all possible scenarios that could develop as a result of this move. Had I gone too far? Overstepped my boundaries? Put my family in jeopardy? Would this move lead to my being investigated? Would the Gestapo be alerted? The French police? Would I have to run away once more? And hide? But where?

My friends and most of the students kept giving me support and reassuring me that they would not back down, that they would "fight" for our cause all the way. Wasn't this the way the French Revolution began, with a handful of citizens banding together all the way to the barricades?

I was summoned alone to the Dean's conference room. Why was I being called to the conference room? Was I being called in front of a panel of judges? A jury? Would I be charged and accused of subversion? Would I be sentenced for sedition? I imagined the worst

Oh, my God. What if they rejected my request?

How would I handle a rejection? How would I face my supporters? How would I handle a defeat, a surrender? But worst of all, a return into the lair of the beast, the Serpent?

Dressed in white shirt and tie, long dark pants and as neat as I pictured any diplomat would look, I walked as confidently as I could to the Dean's conference room.

I entered the huge and solemn room and was awed by the life-size paintings of famous historical figures on all three walls, Louis XIV, Napoleon and Marshall Petain, the carved ceiling, and the long hanging drapes over the twenty foot windows. The smell of tobacco filled the room. As I came into the room, the Dean extended his hand, indicating the leather seat at the end of the huge mahogany conference table.

"Sit down, Bercovici," he said, as he sat down at the other end.

"Bercovici, you have behaved in a most remarkable way!" he said, as he lighted his pipe.

"Yes, Sir. You might say so."

He smiled. "You do realize that you have incited a large group of students and rebelled against an age old, well-established curriculum?"

"Yes, Sir. I do."

I didn't know where he was heading with this but I chose to be cautious and to wait.

"I must say that you are a brave young man and that you show determination in your beliefs."

"Yes, Sir. I believe that there are times when progress must go on," I said, "even if it means changing the old well-established system of doing things."

"Well, you're right. I am happy to tell you that the Curriculum Committee met and approved your request to form a new section."

He paused to see my reaction and went on, "It will be called 'Experimental Sciences' and will start with the new school year in September."

I felt a terrible urge to hug him or even kiss him. I said, "I'm so happy to hear that. And I wish to thank you and the Committee for their support."

"Remember, Bercovici, this is an experiment. In fact, that's why we call it 'Experimental Sciences'. I sincerely hope it works. We'll try it for a year and re-evaluate."

"Thank you, Sir."

I got up and left. I couldn't wait to tell my friends who had invested their confidence in me and who were waiting in the school yard.

As I emerged in the courtyard, a big crowd of students formed around me.

"Well, did you do it?" asked several of my friends in unison.

I said, "We did it. We did it. We won. We won. We'll have our Science class!"

They cheered and yelled "Berco, Berco, Berco…!!! I felt like a man who had won the Presidency of the country!

I learned that if one has a conviction worth fighting for, one should never give up but forge ahead, make plans and stay the course! Just as my mother always said.

26- The Liberation

By mid-1944, life was looking brighter and more promising. As we listened to the BBC, we were getting excited at the thought of being liberated ourselves. For several days Radio London had been sending cryptic messages such as "The apple trees are blooming," "Jean put on your hat," and "The speckled cat has meowed three times." On June 5 there were eight hours of these messages.

On June 6 we heard the wonderful announcement. "This morning at six-thirty, the combined forces…" It was D—Day. Allied troops had landed on French soil and were making huge inroads into the German lines.

Mother and I jumped with joy and excitement.

Five Allied divisions, 7,000 ships and landing craft with 24,000 Americans and British paratroopers constituted the Allied force. The paratroopers arrived first just after midnight and took up positions on the flanks of the invasion beaches. Six hours later, the main assault force landed on beaches code-named Utah, Omaha, Gold, Juno and

Sword. As ships bombarded the German positions, thousands of troops swept ashore.

We stayed close to the radio. We listened to Charles de Gaulle, addressing the people of France. "The supreme battle has begun! After so many battles, so much fury, so much sorrow, the time is here for the decisive confrontation that has been awaited for so long."

* * *

Armed with huge supplies of ammunitions, dynamite, and machine guns, various Resistance guerrilla groups started to destroy German troops and military installations all around Lyon and all major cities. The Germans were incurring major losses not only from invading Allied troops but also from the French Forces of the Interior.

The BBC reported that the Seventh Army of General Patch and the Free French forces under General Jean de Lattre de Tassigny had landed on the beaches of Provence and were on their way to Toulon and Marseille.

On August 15th, we heard more news. American troops and the Free French forces had landed near St Tropez. Although there had been rivalry between American and French generals, their armies had managed to advance with relatively little opposition until they reached an area near Montelimar in the Rhone valley. There, the 11th Panzer division was engaged in fierce fighting, despite heavy Allied air attacks. The Allies kept on moving forward to the north as the Germans were retreating.

In Lyon we knew that things were getting pretty hot because all the German troops were preparing to leave and were blowing up all our bridges behind them. We were excited about their leaving but were worried about the news we had heard that pockets of Germans were planning to stay until the very last minute to cover the rear.

By mid-August, as the Franco-American troops made their way into Provence, major fighting erupted between German troops and the "maquisards" (the men in the maquis.) Military installations were set ablaze. Bridges were blown up. Trains were derailed. Fleeing troops were ambushed or encircled.

By the end of August, word came to us through Uncle David, that Alban Vistel, local F.F.I. Chief, had ordered the maquisards to come out and encircle the whole city of Lyon.

On September 3rd, they joined forces with the First French Division of General Diego Brosset and several American divisions. Lyon was finally liberated.

*   *   *

Liberation Day was a day that will live in my memory. To see Americans and French forces marching down the streets where Germans had goose-stepped days before was a sight I'd never forget.

I remember the radio blaring "The War Is Over; The Germans Have Surrendered; This Is V Day; Rejoice Everybody." I shouted to my mother, "I'm going to City Hall, Mother. That's where they, de Gaulle and the Americans, are going to make speeches. I've got to go. See'ya later."

The sun was warming up the city that was about to explode with excitement.

Filled with joy and exhilaration, I ran until I reached the square in front of City Hall. Thousands of people were gathered, all expecting to see General de Gaulle.

Finally, emotions burst with tears, smiles, laughter, shouts of praise, loud whistles, clapping and dancing.

Several dignitaries: The mayor, city officials, French and American officers joined General de Gaulle on the main balcony of this majestic building overlooking the square. But it wasn't General de Gaulle. It was General Brosset, the general who had led the troops into the city.

The crowd was in total rapture, some jumping with joy, some laughing and dancing, others crying and yelling "Vive la France! Vive la France!"

Suddenly, out of the cacophony of this exuberant crowd, as the general was about to start his speech, we heard shots being fired.

The crowd thought that these were shots from resistance fighters who were joining in the celebration. But as several people were hit and fell to the ground, panic spread. People were running in all directions. We could hear the ra-ta-ta-ta of machine guns spraying bullets all over the square.

I heard shouts and screams "The Germans are shooting! The Germans are shooting! Everybody lay down! Run, run, run…"

Machine guns, like deafening jack hammers, were spraying bullets in all directions. Some people had fallen onto the ground, some dead, others wounded. Screams of people could be heard for a while, then gave way to moans and groans of those hit and wounded, bleeding and writhing in pain. Bright red blood began to stain the pavement and flowed into the gutter. The smell of death was in the air.

I ran as fast as I could, jumping over bodies, bottles, clothes and cartons strewn everywhere. Where was my friend, Serge? Where was Henri? Should I look for them? Had they been shot?

The shooting stopped and silence reigned. It was if this crowd had been smack in the center of a turkey shoot. Bits of clothing, shoes, cigarettes, newspapers, glasses were scattered across the streets in uneven piles. I saw people wounded, trying desperately to limp or crawl to safety into some man holes or into side alleys. I didn't know how and whom to help in this chaos. I didn't know where to turn, whether to keep walking or to remain crouched in a doorway.

I made my way to the sides of a building and I ran, covering my head as if I was in a torrential rain. The shooting resumed.

I decided to take shelter in a dark entry way, squatting and pressing my body as tightly as I could against the doorway, hoping that the shadow would hide me from the shooters.

Bullets were ricocheting on the walls and bouncing all around with brassy deafening sounds. A few people beside me had been hit, screaming in pain, limping or crawling into side streets and still trying to get away from the shooting.

People next to me whispered, "You think they stopped?" The shooting resumed. But this time our Allied forces were shooting back and aiming at the rooftops.

Out of the corner of my eye, I saw some bodies, dressed in green uniform, dropping out of the sky, like limp puppets plummeting to the ground. I could see more blood, more open flesh, more carnage on the ground.

George M. Burnell, M.D.

Guns became silent, replaced by the wailing and moaning of those on the ground. I was confused, dazed, disoriented, and I walked aimlessly, trying not to step on bodies around me. I didn't know if I had been shot and kept checking my arms and legs, looking for blood.

I decided to walk back home, hoping that I would find Mother and Grandfather safe and sound.

As I came into the house, Mother saw that I was covered with blood. She yelled, "Oh, my God! What happened to you? Where are you hurt?"

"I don't think I'm hurt, Maman. It's not my blood," I said.

"What happened, for God's sake, tell me. Let me wash all this blood off," she said.

"German snipers were shooting at City Hall. But we got all of them. I saw them fall from the rooftops. It's over now."

Mother hugged me for several minutes, not wanting to let go, as if she was afraid that I would disappear again from her life.

* * *

Eleven days after Liberation Day, on September 14, de Gaulle came to Lyon and, in a historic speech, paid homage to Lyon, nominating the city as "the capital of the Resistance movement". In doing so, he acknowledged the major role that this city had assumed in the fight against the oppressor.

*   *   *

In Lyon, the Resistance fighters had taken over the radio station and now we were getting breaking news directly about the liberation of other cities throughout France. Mother and I were sitting close to the radio's speaker, exhilarated at the news that Paris had been liberated and saved from destruction. We were getting detailed reports of latest developments in Paris.

It was ironical that de Gaulle, the leader of Fighting France, had not been able to use the French forces for the liberation of France. Although the French armies had numbered 400,000 men, of which 230,000 had been stationed in Algiers, most had been committed to the Allied campaign in Italy.

It was for one of de Gaulle's generals, General Leclerc, commander of the French Second Armored Division, to get the honor of marching into Paris on August 25th, while German artillery was still firing in the distance.

On August 26th, the radio was giving us a thorough account of the events as they were happening. De Gaulle had entered Paris in triumph in the midst of a city overcome with joy, hysterical happiness and overflowing exuberance. Standing rigidly at attention, tall and thin, de Gaulle, wearing the light tan uniform of the French Army, had acknowledged the salute of every passing unit from the reviewing stand. Next to him, stood Lieutenant General Omar Bradley, commander of American ground forces, Generals Hodges and Gerow, Brigadier General Norman D. Cota, Divisional Commander and General Leclerc.

One couldn't help but wonder why Paris had escaped destruction by the Germans. Later, we learned how the sequence of events that had preceded the liberation explained what had happened.

General Dietrich von Choltitz was a Prussian officer who had supervised the destruction of Rotterdam in 1940 and Sebastopol in

1942. When he arrived in Paris in August 1944, Hitler ordered, "Turn Paris into a front-line city; destroy it rather than surrender it to the enemy!"

Pierre Taittinger, the owner of the Taittinger champagne house and the Vichy-appointed mayor of Paris knew that he had to do something—anything—to save it. Police, postal, telephone and railway workers had gone on strike. Barricades had been erected in the streets as the Resistance intensified its plans for insurrection. The Germans became afraid that a full-scale uprising was in the making. Parisians witnessed a most surreal spectacle: dozens of trucks, overcrowded cars and vehicles pulling cannons, ambulances full of wounded trying to pass each other. But the most amazing sight according to Larry Collins and Dominique Lapierre in *Is Paris Burning?* was "Paris being emptied by the truckload. Bathtubs, bidets, rugs, furniture, radios, cases and cases of wine—all rode past the angry eyes of Paris that morning."

Taittinger got an appointment with von Choltitz at the hotel Meurice. Von Choltitz was adamant. If any German was fired at, he would "burn all the houses in that particular block and execute every inhabitant."

Taittinger pleaded with Choltitz to reconsider. "Paris," he said, "is one of the few great cities of Europe that remain intact; you must help me to save it!"

Although Choltitz said that he had his orders, he admitted that he had no personal wish to destroy Paris and that he actually enjoyed looking at the city.

Taittinger took this opportunity to drive his point. "Generals rarely have the power to build, they more often have the power to destroy." He asked Choltitz what it would be like for him to return to Paris some day and be able to say, 'It was I, Dietrich von Choltitz, who, on a certain day, had the power to destroy this but I saved it for humanity.'

Choltitz listened with interest but didn't say what he would do.

Awaiting reinforcements, Choltitz arranged a temporary truce with the Gaullist resistance group, but the truce foundered.

Taittinger returned to his office and waited. Explosives were planted throughout the city. Twenty two thousand troops, mostly SS,

100 tiger tanks and 90 bombers waited for the signal to raze the city. The signal was never given. Von Choltitz had disobeyed Hitler's orders.

Eisenhower, who had planned to bypass Paris to avoid a costly battle, agreed to dispatch General Leclerc's 2nd Free French Armored Division with the support of the US 4th Infantry Division. After Leclerc sent information to Eisenhower about the size of the German forces inside the city, Eisenhower agreed on August 3rd to take the city.

Despite Hitler's pressure to proceed with the destruction of Paris, Choltitz, who had procrastinated, refused to act and surrendered the city intact.

*   *   *

It was a remarkable page in the history of the City of Lights and one for which Parisians should forever be grateful.

On this memorable August 26th, de Gaulle, while riding down the Champs Elysees, waved at half a million hysterically happy Parisians whose emotions could not be contained.

All over Paris bands played lively tunes while the crowds chanted and the men marched in front of tanks rolling slowly behind them.

Thousands of French women were embracing and kissing French troops and American GIs as they were marching down the Champs Elysees. Men were singing the "Marseillaise", while opening champagne, wine and beer bottles for anyone in the streets. Emotions were running high and bubbling throughout the city throughout the night.

Even though the war was not over, the festive spirit was spreading everywhere in France.

27- Dolphy

On December 21, 1944, as we were basking in the joys of liberation, an amazing event took place in our lives.

I had just come back from school and someone knocked at the door.

When I opened the door, I saw a tall, gangly soldier, dressed in a full American uniform, inquiring in broken French, "Je cherche la famille Meyer. Pouvez-vous dire ou est- elle?" (I'm looking for the Meyer family. Can you tell me where they are?)

I barely understood what he was saying, his accent being so foreign. Then, I said, "We are the Meyer family. Just a minute, let me call my mother."

I wondered what in the world would an American soldier want from us? Were we in some kind of trouble with the Americans, too? How could that be possible? I hoped that Mother could handle this touchy situation, like she had so often done others in the past.

Mother came and asked him what he wanted. He answered in German:

"Ich bin Dolphy. Ihre neffe!." (I'm Dolphy, your nephew)

"Oh, mon Dieu," said my mother, overcome with joy, while embracing him.

"George, this is your cousin from America, Dolphy. Remember him. He escaped from Austria and went to America. He and his mother visited us in Paris in 1937, remember?"

Dolphy was still standing in the doorway.

"Please, come in. Come in. Oh! My God. I can't believe my eyes," said Mother.

We all gathered in the living room to hear the whole story.

"I can only stay a few hours," said Dolphy "and forgive me, but it's easier if I speak English," he added as an apology.

We continued our conversation in English. Both my mother and I understood enough English to get by.

"I am with the signal intelligence in the 5th Army. My outfit is in Italy, and I will have to go back later today."

"But how did you find us?" asked Mother in total amazement.

"Well, I drove my jeep to Lyon and asked for a list of dentists in the area. I didn't want to give them a name. Just asked for a list. Then,

I found David's name on the list (his full name was David Distel) and went to the address listed. Neighbors told me he had disappeared and had left no forwarding address.

Mother insisted we all move to the kitchen and she fixed him a sandwich.

We were totally enraptured as he went on with his story. "I ran into a Jewish refugee who was suspicious at first when I told him that I was looking for David Distel, a dentist. But he relaxed when I told him in Yiddish that I was a relative and was here to help the family. Fortunately, he knew David. Actually, he had been one of his patients. Then he told me where I could find him in Bourgoin.

"He said that David was well-known in the Bourgoin area because he had been a hero in the Resistance and a friend of Mr. Cordier, Raoul and Remy, all leaders in the maquis and the Free French Forces.

"When I got there, I pretended that I was a patient with a terrible toothache and that I needed immediate help. He agreed to see me right away."

He took a bite of the sandwich Mother had fixed for him, a swallow of coffee, and resumed his story. "I had been told that David never refused to see a patient in acute pain and always stopped whatever he was doing to attend to the patient in distress. As he was treating a patient in the dental chair at the time, he told the patient to excuse him, because an emergency had just arisen with a new patient.

"He seemed surprised to see an American soldier, but invited me to come and asked no questions. I could no longer carry on the pretense. I looked at David straight in the eye and said, 'do you know, who I am?' He looked shocked. Then suddenly, he said, 'I'll be damned. It's you, Dolphy! You bastard. You're doing this to me!' David had tears in his eyes, and hugged me and patted me on the back. He rescheduled his patient and invited me to his house to see Ethel, Betty and Opa who was visiting for a few weeks."

He paused, took a deep breath and went on. "When Opa saw me in my American soldier's uniform, he said, 'Isn't it strange that he looks so much like a grandson of mine?' And then I said in German, 'Opa, this is your grandson, Dolph!'"

We were all enraptured, smiling and enjoying his narration.

"Later, Betty, who couldn't stop hugging me, took me to the place where you had been staying last summer and gave me your address in Lyon."

This was such a happy experience for all of us. An incredible reunion!

Dolph told us about his fortunate escape from Austria. How he had been one of the 10,000 children who were in the KinderTransport to England in 1938.

He had been one in the first 600 Jewish children to be saved from the Holocaust. The details were now sketchy in his memory. Did he really want to remember this dark period of his life? We didn't press him for details, so we kept quiet and let him tell us just as much as he felt comfortable saying.

He told us how he managed to reach England and after a few months he was re-united with his parents. They obtained their affidavits to the United States from family who had emigrated to the States in the early thirties.

"And what about your parents now, Toni and Eddy?" Mother asked.

"They're both fine. Eddy is working in the plastic business. Mother runs a garment factory in New York. They'll be thrilled to hear news about all of you."

It was getting late and we asked him how much longer he could stay. "I have to leave now, as I am expected back in my unit tonight. I enjoyed meeting all of you. And I hope to see you again some day in the States. Good-bye and stay well."

We all embraced, holding back tears, hugging each other with joy and sadness at the same time.

After his visit to Lyon, Dolph, our American hero, returned to his unit in the 5th Army in Italy. Shortly afterwards, we got word that he had been transferred to Patton's 3rd Army in the Ardennes which was forging ahead in a frantic race to Germany.

28- The Day of Reckoning

Following the liberation, the day of reckoning had arrived for those Frenchmen and women who had collaborated with the Germans. Those who were easily identified and caught had their heads shaved; both men and women were paraded naked in the streets, while the mob was shouting obscenities at them. It was a sorry and barbaric spectacle. A mob lynching. People spitting at them as they were being led to prison. An image of man's cruelty to man that was going to be imprinted on my mind for years. Some of these women had been prostitutes for the Germans. Men, on the other hand, had been informers. In both cases, they were paying a heavy price for having made bad choices.

It was a time of retribution and of settling old scores. About 4,500 persons were summarily executed by tribunals set up by the Resistance.

As purges continued, about 160,000 people were formally charged with collaboration by the new French government and more than

7,000 were condemned to death, but in only 800 cases was the sentence carried out.

An estimated 38,000 were given prison terms.

Top officials of the Vichy government who had collaborated as the "ordinary people" did, often managed to escape or find legal alibis for their misdeeds. What a sad state of affair for those of us who still believed in justice. The higher the people were in the official government, the more chances they had to find a way out, legally or not, of this rat hunt.

In the months following liberation, numerous revelations of horrors of torture, deportation and execution for which the Milice and the Gestapo had been responsible were made public. Many graves of mutilated resistors were discovered in country areas surrounding towns. When cellars of the Gestapo revealed the gruesome secrets of hideous torture, the public demand for legal retribution grew more persistent.

Yet, incidents of injustice, malicious indictments and personal vendettas undoubtedly took place against these collaborators.

The government was worried that the situation was getting out of control and in March 1945, a spokesman for the Minister of Justice announced on the radio that doing business with the enemy did not necessarily constitute a crime. Some of this activity may just be interpreted as "normal" and "legitimate." The government and later the public wanted to "put all this behind us."

Some collaborators did not fare so well. Petain returned from Germany to face the High Court of Justice. He tried to put up a spirited defense. "Every day, a dagger at my throat, I struggled against the enemy's demands," he said. "History will tell all that I spared you, though my adversaries think only of reproaching me for the inevitable...While General de Gaulle carried on the struggle outside our frontiers, I prepared the way for liberation by preserving France, suffering but alive."

Many French agreed with him.

Nevertheless, Petain was found guilty and sentenced to death. Several weeks later, de Gaulle commuted the sentence to life imprisonment. Laval, who was also tried at that time, was found guilty and sentenced to death and executed.

De Gaulle became the hero of the day. Like Eisenhower for the Americans, he commanded respect and was the pride of the nation.

He logically became the leader of the new Republic. He made some bold decisions from the start and decreed that French women should have the right to vote as full citizens, an amazing thing, since the French Revolution had failed to do so almost a century before.

Not only would women vote, but they could also actively engage in the politics of the nation. They had achieved equal rights and equal opportunity in France.

De Gaulle was a unifying force at that time: Communists, socialists, radicals, extreme right, all became French under de Gaulle. After the honeymoon period which lasted a few months, political parties resumed their rivalries, and de Gaulle had to form his own party.

* * *

Life seemed to have returned to normal after Liberation. Allied forces were still fighting their way into Germany, but everyone knew that it was just a matter of time before Nazi Germany would collapse.

At the college, I became part of a small group of boys, more like a clique, who were too few to be considered a gang. We called ourselves, "the new French Avant-Guard" although we had no real political recognition or ambition. Jacques Peju, a tough looking young man with long sideburns, a pointed chin, and a commanding voice, became the titular head of the group. There were about seven of us, all with towering hair, as was the style of the time, always dressed with long pants, dark shirt, coat and slim white tie, to distinguish ourselves from the low-class boys across town who relished loitering in overalls and tattered clothes.

Rivalry existed between several gangs, but we always held our head high and our shoulders straight to show that we were proud and confident, fearless, and intellectually superior in our opinion. Besides, we knew that some members of these gangs had been German sympathizers and collaborators, and that gave us more justification for opposing them.

Jacques held a black belt in judo which was just beginning to be known as an elite sport and art in self-defense. It was not long before I learned this martial art that would give me self-confidence and leadership in the future.

I joined the new "dojo" (judo club) and became a favorite of the Japanese teacher Professor Hayashi. I progressed steadily, learning the various katas (routines of self defense sequences) and passed all the belt exams including the brown belt preceding the black belt. I felt proud and extremely confident, no longer having any fears of being cornered or assailed by anyone. What a great feeling!

One of my fondest memories is when I was assailed by a gang member in a lonely side street. It was on a summer afternoon when everyone seemed to be out of town or away at seaside resorts.

A tall, lanky, gangly teenager, disheveled, dressed with dirty overalls and rat-bitten sneakers, stood in the middle of the street, hands on his hips, blocking my path. I imagined that he was one who had escaped the community's raid on collaborators.

Without wasting any time, he yelled the usual provocative insults, "You punks. You all think you're superior. Well, come on and prove it," he said while spitting and snarling, itching for a fight.

In Strasbourg a few years ago, groups of Alsatian boys had surrounded me, stones in their hands, asking me to kneel down and accept a volley of insults and indignities.

This time, I was armed with all my knowledge and skill of judo and self-defense. I stood there with my arms stretched out, inviting him to come closer, my eyes firmly locked into his gaze. Although I could sense a mild hesitation in his eyes, he seemed unwilling to flinch or retreat.

How ridiculous to be caught in this show of male chauvinistic rivalry. We had to show each other and the world who was superior, fearless and in command. By his appearance, I judged that he was from one of the collaborator gangs my friends and I had identified and pledged to fight.

I knew that time was critical, because sooner or later, he would be joined by the rest of his gang, and if I waited much longer my only chance for survival would be a fast retreat.

George M. Burnell, M.D.

This was a unique opportunity to prove myself and to show to my own group that I had what it took to hold my own.

Like a toreador teasing his bull to come closer and closer, I was moving my arms in a rhythmic fashion in front of me, while nodding my head, encouraging him to come nearer. Sensing that it would not be an easy fight, he drew a switch blade and dared me to approach him.

The street was deserted. Laundry on clothes lines in the windows above our heads was flapping in the breeze. The street was still and silent. He came closer and lunged ahead with the knife aiming at my groin. In a typical judo maneuver, I quickly stepped aside, caught his arm on the fly, and lifting him over my shoulder with a circular motion, propelled his body over my head until he landed on the edge of the curb. The knife went flying out of his hands into the gutter.

He let out a loud scream and was unable to move. I became frightened. Had I broken his spine? Would he be paralyzed? What should I do? Help him? Run? A few heads peered out of windows above us and some people shouted, "What the hell are you boys doing?"

I asked him. "Can you move?"

"I'm not sure. You punk. I'll get you for this."

I couldn't afford to play the good Samaritan, knowing that his friends would appear any minute.

"I hope you feel better soon," I said and ran off.

When my avant-guard group heard about the episode, Jacques appointed me as his proxy when he was out of town. I had arrived in this new world of young Turks.

29- The Papon Affair

We didn't hear any news about Papa until we were notified by the Red Cross in 1945. A letter found its way to Mr. Broca, the lawyer in Bordeaux, who later forwarded it to us in Lyon.

The letter said that Mr. Andre Meyer had been identified as one of the victims in Auschwitz. Specifically, he had been transported on convoy number 65, and had died on June 23rd, 1943.

The official letter ended with an expression of sincere condolences.

The reality of his death didn't sink in until I read over and over again the letter from the Red Cross.

His memory haunted me. I wondered what could have saved him? Why did he refuse to come along with us when we fled Bordeaux? We had hidden paratroopers in our cellars, so what did he expect? We must have been high on the Gestapo list of suspects so how could he have been so naive?

I became obsessed with other questions What was it like for him in Auschwitz? I had read early accounts of the concentration camp experience, but they seemed so unbelievable that it was hard for me to accept them.

I continued to ruminate over the Holocaust experience, especially when I realized that I had narrowly escaped a similar fate myself. I spoke to several survivors I met over the last five decades, always wondering what the experience was like. Most were reticent to talk about it, including Betty's husband, Fred, whom I got to know later in the States.

I read several books by authors who had been in Auschwitz or Buchenwald: "All the Rivers Run to the Sea: Memoirs" by Elie Wiesel; "Of Blood and Hope" by Samuel Pisar; "Life or Literature" by Jorge Semprun., "A Link in the Chain" and "The Healing Echo" by Eugene Heimler, "The Uprooted" by Dorit Bader Whiteman, "I remember..." by Dr. Dov Weissberg, who had lost his entire family and is now a renown cardiovascular surgeon in Israel.

I was looking for answers. What did my father endure? What for? The only answer I found is that War begets Evil and Evil begets War. It's that simple. And when one is caught in this madness, only death will deliver one from relentless suffering.

The other option is survival at a heavy price: loss of human dignity, relegation to animal instincts and most basic and primitive traits and with hope as the only remaining human emotion. And hope was the only thing we held on to, so tightly, that it pulled us through the deepest and darkest pits of despair.

But those of us who were able to "smell" a rat, who suspected the enemy's evil motives and who mistrusted those in power, were rewarded with the promise of survival.

* * *

Whereas the trials of German Nazi war criminals at Nuremberg lasted ten months and ended in 1946, the trials of French Nazi leaders were delayed, protracted and obfuscated for years.

It is ironic that the man who sent my papa to Auschwitz was alive in 1998, still awaiting the decision of an Appeals Court in the longest trial in the history of France.

Maurice Papon, a collaborator, had been promoted to a high official post in the Vichy government. As the Chief of Police in

Bordeaux, he had signed the deportation papers of 1690 Jews who had been arrested and sent to their deaths in Auschwitz.

Despite a shady history of collaboration, Papon had been able to make a transition from the Vichy government to the Fourth and Fifth Republic administration that was to follow the Liberation.

He became budget director under Giscard d'Estaing, who eventually lost the election against Francois Mitterand, and because of his good pre-war record and connections, he was able to continue getting promotions in subsequent administrations.

Thus, he held posts of prefect in Corsica in 1947, then prefect of Constantine (Algeria) in 1948, and police prefect of Paris in 1958 at a time when France was deeply involved in the war against Algerian independence.

The "Papon Affair" opened on May 6, 1981. Papon had been charged with "crimes committed against humanity", but it wasn't until thirty individuals and several groups had pursued their complaints relentlessly that he was indicted on January 19, 1983.

For several years, Papon, thanks to his lawyers, had been able to side-step all the allegations that were brought against him.

Finally, the trial in the Appeals Court began on October 8, 1997, and lasted six months.

Papon was 87 years old and still awaiting the decision of the High Court. It finally came on April 2, 1998, seventeen years after the initial charges had been brought against him.

The jury after 19 hours of deliberation asked for a sentence of 10 years of prison, but the judgment was appealed. It wasn't until April, 1999, that a final decision was reached by the Appeals court, upholding the sentence of 10 years.

Papon, the collaborator, was still living in his house at Greits-Armainvilliers in the county of Seine-et-Marne in total freedom, while his lawyers were busy preparing the next brief for his defense.

Papon said that he had used his position to save the French people from the Germans and that he had served as an undercover agent for the Resistance.

Imagine a trial for a war criminal that spanned seventeen years and lasted six months of court appearances, the longest in modern history of the French judicial system!

As the proceedings dragged on year after year, emotions had run high among the prosecutors and the defense. The French public was deeply divided over the outcome of this trial. Some felt that Papon was just a pawn of history, but relatives of victims felt differently.

As one of the victim's relative concluded, "For Papon to go to prison will not bring back our loved ones, but only a guilty verdict will save the honor of France and will make Papon understand our pain which he has never acknowledged."

Another added, "I don't give a damn now. I am glad it's over. I am tired of nightmares, of sobbing each night after a day in court. Maybe, what counts is that history will have recorded the true role of Vichy, France."

I, too, had struggled with nightmares which in time became less and less frequent, although, years later, unforgiving thoughts still cross my mind from time to time.

On October 21, 1999, I was dismayed to hear the latest news about Papon. Although he had been found guilty and had been sentenced by the High French Court to ten years in prison, despite his age of 89, he could not be found anywhere.

People suspected that he had fled to Switzerland. But how could this have happened? Wasn't he under surveillance by the French authorities, given his status of a high profile suspect, a war criminal subjected to the longest trial in French history?

Over six years of trials, appeals and retrials under the greatest degree of suspicion, now Papon was on the lam, for the entire world to see! It was the ultimate embarrassment and shame for France.

A few days after Papon's disappearance, the government of Switzerland announced that Papon had been located in a small village and that he was going to be extradited to France. The French people breathed a sigh of relief.

Within days, Papon was arrested by the French police and subsequently transferred to the fortress-like prison of La Santé in Paris.

Yet, after his transfer, it was deemed that this old man was too ill to go to prison and would have to be transferred to a medical facility. His lawyers were still trying to get some protection for him under the law!

Finally, in December 1999, I picked up a magazine that had a small column on Papon. It said that he had been transferred to the prison "Fresnes" outside of Paris.

Nothing was said about his condition, his sentence or his state of mind. Lawyers, however, had been able to provide him with a blanket of privacy, relatively comfortable living conditions and total medical care.

On January 19, 2001, I read in the New York Times that Papon's lawyers were pleading for his release from prison, claiming that at an advanced age of 90, there would be "nothing to be gained from his completing his 10 year sentence."

Turned down by President Jacques Chirac, Papon's lawyers appealed to the European Court of Human Rights, claiming that his continued incarceration violated a ban by the European Convention on Human Rights on inhuman and degrading treatment. However, his lawyer, Mr. Robert Badinter, a former justice minister, whose father had died in a German concentration camp, said that only Jacques

George M. Burnell, M.D.

Chirac had the authority to release Papon. Incidentally, under French law, Papon would have been eligible for parole in 2004!

Again, there was outrage and pain among the survivors who had suffered from these decisions. The issue became a basis for debates in editorials of all the newspapers. Politicians spoke on both sides of the issue. "This brings up the larger issue of how do we deal with aged and dying convicts in our justice system," said Elizabeth Guigou, the justice minister of the Socialist-led government. Alain Levy, another lawyer, raised more questions, "Should all older prisoners be released because of advanced age? Should it matter that Papon successfully avoided jail for years because of legal tactics? No," said Levy.

Should we ever forget that Papon was the highest ranking French official who was convicted for having helped deport thousands of men, women, and children to Nazi concentration camps, while he was chief of police in Bordeaux? I never will.

When my step-father was arrested in 1942, his lawyer was helpless and unable to intervene in the French justice system.

Mr. Broca, the well-known and influential lawyer in Bordeaux was totally ignored in the Vichy judicial system.

How does anyone come to terms with the injustice of a justice system? The answer is that there is no viable justice system under a totalitarian government that is implementing a policy of extermination of an entire group of people deemed inferior.

A significant number of the French people had collaborated with the Germans, had adopted their policies, and had bought into the new justice system. They didn't care that Jews would be the sacrificial lambs and that they would be the price to pay for such a peace.

Wasn't it ironical that out of the top four French war criminals (Laval, Bousquet, Papon and Touviers) none except Laval was brought to justice because each managed "to disappear or die of natural causes?"

History is filled with acts of cruelty and inhumanity to Man never brought to justice. I think that major war crimes are punished only when it is politically expedient to those in power. Isn't this true for WWII, Korea, Vietnam, the Israeli wars, Chechnia, Desert Storm, Bosnia, Kosovo, Afghanistan, all in our times?

And isn't it true for the Roman and Grecian wars, the cruel and bloody conquests by the Barbarians, the Crusaders, the Ottoman and

Islamic armies, the Napoleonic armies, the American, French and Russian revolutions, the Civil War, the two World Wars, all bathed in blood and littered with pounds of flesh and broken skulls and bones, but never cleansed by contrition, restitution or atonement.

The bottom truth remains, as always, that we learn <u>about</u> history but <u>not</u> from history!

30- Miriam

Mother sold both restaurants in Bordeaux and announced that it was time to move on. "There were better business opportunities in Paris," she said.

We moved to Paris, and within a few weeks, Mother had bought a new restaurant with spacious living quarters upstairs. It was located on the Boulevard de Port Royal, a few blocs from the Latin Quarter and the Luxembourg Gardens. I enrolled for my last year at the College Arago and made a new set of friends.

Life seemed to have resumed the old routine. I bartended after finishing my homework, and Mother seemed happy meeting new customers and neighbors.

Mother got a call from a family, seeking to rent an apartment. They were refugees from Czechoslovakia who needed to stay in Paris while waiting for their U.S. visa. Mother said that they would be good renters and accepted them right away.

This new development was to bring a major change in my life after I discovered that the Shapshovitz family had an attractive daughter named Miriam. The family had survived a year in the concentration camp in Therezinstadt and were eager to start a new life in the U.S. Their immigration documents were being processed in Paris, and the waiting period was estimated to be about six months.

Miriam was a vivacious girl, well-endowed with blooming femininity and warmth. She had hazel eyes, long flowing silky auburn hair and a smile that radiated happiness. I couldn't take my eyes off her gracious figure showing through her silk dress, as she walked voluptuously up and down the street.

Our eyes had locked onto each other on several occasions. We had felt a magic spark between us and our hands like powerful magnets were pulling them together. Her charms were disarming. It was not long before we couldn't keep our hands off each other. In her sexy, delicious voice graced with a velvety Czech accent that sounded just like Za Za Gabor, she confided in me and said. "If djou vill blay jess viz my fazer, he vill like you better."

I was delighted to hear this. I am an avid chess player.

She arranged to set up a game between her father and me after dinner. I lost that first game quickly, although I had maintained a better position during most of the game. Miriam, watching the game, did not help my concentration. We played two more games which I lost despite several spectacular moves I was proud of.

Miriam smiled and consoled me the rest of the evening and that brought me as much pleasure as I would have had if I had won.

Her father and I began to play regularly before dinner and then after dinner. Later, we played after lunch and more on the weekends.

I rarely won, but I didn't mind because my romance with Miriam was meeting with the approval of both sets of parents. What else could I ask?

I couldn't win in chess but I was willing to settle for humility on the chess board in exchange of pleasures after dark. That was a small price to pay for a passionate romance. And there was no ultimatum from Miriam, from her parents or from my mother.

After everyone had gone in bed, I'd sneak out of my room and find a warm welcome in Miriam's bed. We had to be careful not to giggle too loudly, as her parents were in the next room, separated only by a thin wall.

"You are nice to blay wiz my fazer," she whispered.

"Yes, I know. But I never win. I don't understand why I can never win."

"Well, my fazer, he is very good. He is the champion of all Czechoslovakia!"

I was dumbfounded. Now, I understood my plight. I was learning to play well, but at the cost of swallowing my male pride every single day!

"I vill blay jess wiz you, George," she said with a consoling tone of voice, knowing how much my male pride had been hurt.

"All right," I said, hoping that she would still respect my manhood. After all, that was—I thought at the time—the most important thing to me.

Miriam and I began to play chess, and for some reason, I would win most of the time. But then, perhaps she let me win out of pity for me.

Was that the way men women relationships were supposed to be?

That one or the other would have to feel pity for the other so the relationship could survive? I did appreciate her motherly warmth and constant reassurance. She was aware of the bruising that my ego was suffering each day after the repeated humiliation on the chess board. It was as if I was receiving several lashes at each game, and to make matters worse, both families always asked about the result of the games at the end of the day.

The visas for the Shapshovitz family arrived. It was time to say good-bye. I was heartbroken because I felt unsure that we were ever going to see each other again.

"I vill vait for you in New York, George!"

"I love you, Miriam, and I'll come to America. Please wait for me." We kissed passionately once more before I was to play one last game with her father.

We played that game on the eve before they left for America. At the end of that game he said to me in broken French, "Jamais seras un grand champion, mais seras un tres bon joueur (You'll never be a champion, but you'll be a very good player)."

I took that as the biggest compliment anyone had ever made to me on my intellectual abilities, but I wondered if I could ever marry Miriam and live with being emasculated by her father every week for the rest of my life!

Yet, I hoped that I would see her again in New York some day. But would I be willing to leave France, my friends and forgo my plans of becoming a doctor in Paris? I wasn't sure and didn't know where my destiny would lead me.

Four years later, when Miriam and I met again, this time in mid-Manhattan, she told me, tears streaming down her cheeks, that she married a jeweler, and that she was sorry and...

* * *

On May 8, 1945, half an hour before midnight, the German High Command in Berlin signed the agreement of surrender. The war in Europe, which had lasted five years and eight months was over.

I was a child playing with toys when the war started and going on sixteen when it ended. Like thousands of French Jewish teenagers, my growing years were filled with episodes of fear and terror, which would remain dormant and buried inside for years to come.

Epilogue

Like so many Jewish European families, my family's dispersal throughout the world was a micro re-enactment of the Diaspora.

My father fled from Rumania to settle in France. He ran from persecution and discrimination in search of freedom and a chance to succeed in life. He survived the war and died in 1954 from stomach cancer.

My mother left Austria (once Polish territory) to settle in France. She was seeking a country where women could pursue their dreams without restraint. She immigrated to the U.S. in 1955, owned and managed several rest homes until she died at the age of 89 from heart and Alzheimer's disease.

My French step-father, who escaped from German POW camps, later became one of the first victims in Auschwitz after his arrest in Bordeaux. He died in 1943.

Aunt Ethel left Austria to seek the promise of a better future in France. She married David, and both immigrated to the U.S. She died from ovarian cancer at the age of ninety.

Uncle David fled from Poland because of discrimination and anti-Semitism to study dentistry and start a family in France. He taught and practiced in Paris before and after the war. He left France with Ethel and Betty, his daughter, hopeful of a new beginning in the United States. He re-graduated from the University of Montreal, Canada, School of Dentistry and practiced and taught dentistry in New York until his death from prostate cancer at the age of seventy five.

Betty, my cousin, went to Hunter College, obtained a Master's degree in French literature, then attended dental school for two years. She married Fred Sterzer, a scientist, and lived in Princeton until she succumbed to breast cancer at the age of sixty.

Betty's husband, Freddy, fled from Austria to the U.S. after liberation from a concentration camp and losing his entire family in the Holocaust. He became head of the RCA Research Laboratory in Princeton, N.J. and later established his own consulting firm in the same town. He holds numerous invention patents in the field of microwaves and cancer research.

Uncle David's cousins escaped Nazi raids in Poland and settled in Israel.

Grandfather Opa and Grandmother Oma slipped out of Austria to France to avoid deportation to concentration camps. Oma died in a bombing raid in Bordeaux. Opa later came to the U.S. where he died in a New York hospital.

Uncle Eddy, Toni and Cousin Dolph fled from Austria to England and later to the U.S. to escape Nazi Germany. They owned and managed a successful garment factory in New York city. Eddy lived into his nineties and Toni died in her eighties from complications of cardiovascular disease.

Uncle Deje, Aunt Ria and Cousin Lothar emigrated from Austria to Uruguay to elude the Nazis. They died in Montevideo and are survived by their son, Lothar, a practicing dentist.

Uncle Adi ran away from Austria's Nazis to Portugal and later to the U.S., where he joined the Navy. A few years later, he was killed in a car accident in New York.

After surviving WWII, I, too, followed a similar escape route. I left France, my country of birth, to avoid getting into a senseless war in Vietnam, clearly in conflict with my convictions, values and goals in life. At 20, I immigrated to the U.S. in 1950, attended pre-med and medical school at Columbia University and served in the United States Air Force Medical Corps as a psychiatrist. Later, I worked as an emergency room physician while finishing a residency in psychiatry. Later, I completed a career in psychiatry, serving as Chief of Psychiary at Kaiser Permanente, the largest HMO in the country, and raised an American family.

History kept repeating itself for this family, generation after generation. But I discovered later that it was probably typical of many such families in Europe.

The Austrian branch and the Polish branch of my family broke away to flee the prospect of being annihilated.

The French branch left France to seek peace, security, and greater opportunity in the U.S.

Being uprooted from one's native land and cast into a sea of uncertainty and thrust into a shadowy future and a foreign culture and lifestyle, has been the fate of thousands of Jewish families in Europe in this century. Yet their fate has been no different from those families who had preceded them in the previous twenty centuries, as far back as Egyp and Rome.

Despite great upheavals in the world's history against foreigners and Jews in particular, there have been times of great stability in Poland, Russia, Rumania, Turkey, Lebanon, Czechoslovakia, Hungary, Germany, Italy, Austria and France.

Between these periods of calm and peace, families had to survive periods of political upheavals, revolutions, inquisitions, wars, progroms. ghettos, and even genocide.

My family and I had to find ways of surviving during these intermissions of the ongoing drama of history while others, more unfortunate, perished under the heavy hand of destiny.

In the end, I think that it is truly a wonder of the human spirit that people, when thrown into pits of despair, can rise against all odds and create a life of hope and meaning.

General Petain and Cardinal Gerlier, 1942: Coll. A. Gamet

German Trooops Marching Into Lyon, November 8, 1942: D.M.I.H. (D.R.)

Changing of the Guards at the Grand Hotel, Lyon, 1943: D.M.I.H. (D.R.)

German Troops Entering Lyon, November 8, 1942: D.M.I.H. (D.R.)

**German Troops Re-Entering Lyon, November 11, 1942: Ministere des Anciens
Combatants et Victimes de Guerre- D.M.I.H. (D.R.)**

German Motorized Troops in Lyon: Coll. A. Gamet

Massacres of Summer 1944: S.R.I.J. (D.R.)

**Massacre of Seven Jews at Rillieux-La-Pape Ordered by
Paul Touviers, June 29, 1944: S.R.I.J. (D.R.)**

Resistance Fighters Outside of Lyon: Coll. R. Chavanet, 1944

Bombing of Lyon, May 26, 1944: Coll. A. Gamet

Blowing Up Bridges in Lyon: Coll. A. Gamet and D.M.I.H. (D.R.)

Bridges Destroyed: D.M.I.H. (D.R.)

**American Army Convoy, 7th Army Under Command of
Gerneral Patch, Entering Lyon, September 1944: Coll. A. Gamet**

General De Gaulle, Lyon, 1944: Coll. H. Drevon

Purging of Collaborators, September 3rd, 1944

Purging of Collaborators, Mob Scene, 1944: Coll. A. Gamet

George M. Burnell, M.D.

Bibliography

Aubrac. Raymond. *The French Resistance 1940-1944,* Pocket Archives, Paris: Hazan, 1997.

Collins, Larry and Dominique Lapierre. *Is Paris Burning?* London: Pan Books, 1974.

Davidson, Phillip B. *Vietnam at War, The History 1946-1975,* New York/ Oxford: University Press, Oxford 1988.

de Saint Marc, Helie with Laurent Beccaria. *Les Sentinellles du Soir,* Paris: Editions des Arenes, 1999.

Gilbert, Martin. *The Day the War Ended, May 8, 1945—Victory in Europe,* New York: Henry Holt and Co., 1995.

Golsan, Richard J. ed. *Memory, The Holocaust, and French Justice, The Bousquet and Touvier Affairs,* Hanover and London: University Press of New England, 1996.

Heimler, Eugene. *A Link in the Chain,* Calgary: The University of Calgary Printing Services, 1980.

Jennings, Peter, and Todd Brewster. *The Century,* New York: Doubleday, 1998.

George M. Burnell, M.D.

Kedward, H.R.. *Occupied France: Collaboration and Resistance,* 1940-1944. Oxford: Blackwell Publishers, Historical Association Studies, 1985.

Kladstrup, Don, and Petie Kladstrup with Dr. J. Kim Munholland. *Wine and War: The French, the Nazis, and the Battle for France's Greatest Treasure,* New York, Broadway Books, 2001

Miller, Robert A. *August 1944, The Campaign for France,* Novato: Presidio, 1996.

Netanyahu, Benjamin. *A Place Among the Nations, Israel and the World,* New York: Bantam Books, 1993.

Paxton, Robert O. *Vichy France: Old Guard and New Order, 1940-1944,* New York: Columbia University Press, Morningside Edition, 1982.

Rulliere, Maurice. *Resistance en Bas Dauphine, Histoire du Secteur VII, Liberation de Bourgoin et de Jallieu,* Lyon: Bellier Press, 1942.

Schoenbrun, David. *Soldiers of the Night: The Story of the French Resistance.* New York: New American Library, 1980.

Semprun, Jorge. *Literature or Life,* New York: Viking, 1997.

Szpilman, Wladyslaw. *The Pianist*, New York: Picador USA, 1999.

Weissberg, Dov. *"I Remember...,"* Tel Aviv, Israel, Freund Publishing House, LTD, 1998

Wheal, Elizabeth-Ann, Stephen Pope, and James Taylor. *Encyclopedia of the Second World War*, Edison, New Jersey: Castle Books, 1989.

Whiteman, Dorit Bader. *The Uprooted, A Hitler Legacy/ Voices of Those Who Escaped before the "Final Solution"*, New York: Insight Books/Plenum Press, 1993.

Wiesel, Elie. *All Rivers Run to the Sea/Memoirs*, New York: Schocken Books, 1995.

Zeitoun, Sabine and Dominique Foucher. *Lyon: La Guerre, L'Occupation. La Liberation 1940-1944,* Rennes: Editions Ouest-France, 1994.

About the Author

George M. Burnell, M.D. was born and grew up in France until he immigrated to the United States at the age of twenty. After serving in the USAF (MC) as a Captain he moved to California to raise his family.

He is a graduate of the College of Physicians and Surgeons, Columbia University and the Langley Porter Neuropsychiatric Institute in San Francisco. He is a Diplomate of the American Board of Psychiatry and a Fellow of the American Psychiatric Association.

He is Chief Emeritus of Psychiatry at the Kaiser Permanente Medical Center in Honolulu, Hawaii and former Clinical Assistant Professor of Psychiatry at Stanford University, Palo Alto, California, the John A. Burns School of Medicine, University of Hawaii. He is the author of many scientific articles and two previous books. He lives with his wife in La Quinta, California.

Printed in the United States
6359